YVAIN

OR

THE KNIGHT WITH THE LION

CHRÉTIEN DE TROYES

YVAIN

OR

THE KNIGHT WITH THE LION

TRANSLATED BY

RUTH HARWOOD CLINE

THE UNIVERSITY OF GEORGIA PRESS

ATHENS

FOREWORD

Here, at last, is an excellent translation in very readable English verse of *Yvain; or, Le chevalier au lion* by Chrétien de Troyes. Although this poem is generally regarded as Chrétien's best work, it is not so well known to English readers as his *Conte del Graal* (Perceval) and his *Chevalier de la Charette* (Lancelot), which later poets have so often reworked. It may seem strange that *Yvain*, which was immediately translated into various other languages—including Middle High German and Welsh—was not also put into English at once; for after all it is generally agreed that Chrétien was the best French writer of his time, that he wrote the first-known Arthurian romance, and that he created the genre. The reason for this apparent neglect is perhaps that in the twelfth century, when the poem was written, French was the language of the royal court and of the educated classes in England and that, consequently, an English translation would have been less comprehensible to them than the original. On the other hand, in the fourteenth century, when French was no longer so generally spoken in England, Chaucer, who was a fine connoisseur of Old French literature, might well have translated poems of Chrétien; but instead he chose the *Roman de la rose*, which was the most famous and the most admired French book of *his* time. Then in the fifteenth century, Malory (with Caxton's help) translated and rearranged parts of the enormously long and enormously impressive French prose romances which had developed from the courtly epics of Chrétien. Thanks to his *Morte d'Arthur*, stories of King Arthur, Lancelot, the Holy Grail, and so forth survived in England down through the Renaissance, although in France the older literature was completely eclipsed by works of classical antiquity. And when the manuscripts of Old French were rediscovered and published in the nineteenth century, the scholars who published them were much less interested in the art of medieval poets than in origins, sources, folklore, dialects, etymologies, lexicography, historical grammar, and so on. Consequently the reading public had to wait until the brink of the twentieth century for translations of Chrétien de Troyes even into modern French.

Ruth Harwood Cline's translation is a remarkable literary achievement. She has not only understood Chrétien's difficult and subtle text—which is no small matter, but she frequently succeeds in re-creating his witty style, his irony, his playfulness, his masterful use of octosyllabic couplets which, in his hands, can gallop or meander or creep, depending upon the matter being treated. Sometimes her version even suggests his varied and effortless use of rhymes—now rich, now mere vowel rhyme, now an arresting use of homonyms, now a play on words. And she has studiously avoided archaisms, which are the bane of so many translators. In a word she has made much of the quality of Chrétien's masterpiece available in present-day English.

The reader should bear in mind, however, that Chrétien was the most sophisticated writer of a very sophisticated period. With a sure touch he combined classic themes with Celtic motifs, comedy and tragedy, idealism and realism, sentimentality and irony, solemnity and clowning, pagan magic and Christian beliefs, naive characters with worldly-wise ones, a grand conception of the knight's responsibility to society and a down-to-earth portrayal of human frailty. But however sophisticated it may be, Chrétien's art is somewhat like that of a medieval weaver of tapestries: the first time one looks at a tapestry of the period, he sees a jumble of trees, flowers, animals, people, buildings. Only on closer study does he realize that the medieval conception of perspective was very different from ours, and only then do the different objects seem to fall into place.

The reader should also be warned that medieval literature was written to be declaimed or read aloud, and that it has little in common with books that are written for speed reading. Of course the story itself can be readily grasped by a rapid reading; but the speed reader will miss the different levels of meaning: the genial gallery of portraits Chrétien created (Kay, Guinevere, Lunette, Laudine, Yvain, Gawain, the hermit, even the grateful lion), the atmosphere he quickly conjured up for each scene, whether at court, in country houses, in the forests, or on the road. For example, when Laudine, the grande dame, first talks with

Yvain, she sounds like a grande dame; but when she talks with the maiden Lunette about that glamorous knight, their conversation sounds like the chatter of teen-age girls of all times.

In Mrs. Cline's translation, the reader will find the real Chrétien as he wrote eight hundred years ago, without the traditional gingerbread Gothic decor of "many-tower'd Camelot"—all of which would have greatly surprised our twelfth-century poet. Here, in the words of Ariosto, are "Le donne, i cavalier, l'arme, gli amori, / Le cortesie" as Chrétien created them. So, as Calogrenant says, in the present translation (lines 141–144):

> Now listen! and before I start,
> give me your hearing and your heart,
> for words will quickly disappear,
> if they aren't heard in heart *and* ear.

JULIAN HARRIS

Madison, Wisconsin

ACKNOWLEDGMENTS

While it would be impossible to thank everyone who assisted me during the preparation of this translation, I would like to express my deepest gratitude to Professor Julian Harris for his foreword and for his critical reading of the text. I am very grateful to my former professor of translation, Patricia Terry of Barnard College, for her expert advice and sustained interest in *Yvain*; to Brian Head, the Ford Foundation Visiting Professor of Linguistics in Rio de Janeiro, for reading the manuscript and advising me; and to Mr. J. Martin Harvey of São Paulo, for making important stylistic criticisms and for lending me his books. I thank Professors Henri Peyre, Roger Shattuck, and Eugène Vinaver for their letters of encouragement and advice, and my former professors Albert Wolohojian of Rutgers University and W. T. H. Jackson of Columbia University whose courses at Rutgers sparked my interest in Chrétien de Troyes.

I am most grateful to my husband William R. Cline for his unfailing support and encouragement at every stage of the preparation of this translation, which is dedicated to him.

RUTH HARWOOD CLINE

Washington, D.C.

INTRODUCTION

Chrétien de Troyes was the creator of the Arthurian romance as a literary genre: he was the first known writer in Western Europe to put the Celtic legends of King Arthur and his knights into the long romance form in order to illustrate themes from the twelfth-century codes of love and chivalry. His five romances, *Erec and Enide*, *Cligès*, *Lancelot*, *Yvain*, and *Perceval*, were written between 1160 and 1190, a period in France of great interest in British legends and folklore. Chrétien was considered an outstanding poet in an exceptionally rich period of literary creativity, and his romances were sensationally successful in the courts of Western Europe and Italy and were translated and imitated into the fifteenth century. Apart from their profound influence upon European literature, Chrétien's romances are outstanding in themselves, as poetry, as well-constructed and entertaining tales of love and adventure, as perceptive studies of human psychology and emotion, and as portraits of mankind's struggle to attain the earthly ideals of self-perfection and joy.

What information we have about Chrétien de Troyes is based more upon deduction and conjecture than upon fact. Possibly the same Christianus who was made canon of St. Loup in 1173, Chrétien was probably born in Troyes, where he received a classical education as part of his training as a clerk. He began his literary career by translating and adapting Ovid's *Ars amatoria*, *Remedia amoris*, and two tales from the *Metamorphoses*, "Shoulder Bite" and "Philomena." He may have visited England, perhaps in the train of Henry of Blois, who was appointed abbot of Glastonbury (an abbey noted for strong Arthurian traditions) in 1126 and Bishop of Winchester in 1129. In any case Chrétien became aware of the Arthurian legends, and after composing a tale of Mark and Iseut, based upon the Tristan legends, he wrote *Erec and Enide*, the oldest Arthurian romance, around 1160 and signed it "Chrétien de Troyes," which would indicate that he was not living in Troyes at that time. His later romances are signed "Chrétien." Probably he returned to Troyes soon afterward, where he entered the service of

Countess Marie of Champagne (daughter of Louis VII and Eleanor of Aquitaine). There he composed *Cligès*, a romance with Byzantine overtones which reflects the Tristan legend, and, around 1172, *Lancelot*, with its theme of the adulterous love between Lancelot and Queen Guinevere which was suggested by Countess Marie herself. Between 1173 and 1176 he completed *Yvain* and possibly *Guillaume d'Angleterre;* his authorship of the latter work is heavily disputed. In 1181 Chrétien left the service of the widowed Countess Marie and entered the service of Count Philippe of Flanders, at whose bidding in 1182 he began his last and longest romance, *Perceval* or *The Story of the Grail*. He died before *Perceval* was completed.

Yvain; or, the Knight with the Lion is often considered to be Chrétien de Troyes's masterpiece, and it is one of the best constructed, most captivating tales in medieval literature. The story of the lord Yvain, his beautiful wife, and his devoted lion was carried as far north as Iceland and is preserved in seven manuscripts (Paris B.N. 794, Guiot copy; Paris B.N. 1433; Paris B.N. 1450; Paris B.N. 12560; Paris B.N. 12603; Rome Vatican 1725, Chantilly 432) and two fragments (Montpellier and Annonay). This romance has maintained its high place in medieval literature, not only because of its dramatic adventures, fine analyses of sentiment, and appealing themes, but also because of its poetic language and vivid style.

In the first part of the romance, after hearing his cousin Calogrenant's account of a disastrous visit to a magic, storm-making fountain, the courageous lord Yvain establishes his reputation at King Arthur's court by riding alone to the fountain, braving the storm, slaying the defender of the fountain, and with the help of a maiden, Lunette, marrying the knight's beautiful and wealthy widow. After entertaining King Arthur and the court in his new domain, Yvain receives his wife's permission to leave her, and promising to return within one year, he departs with his friend Gawain to achieve even greater successes at a round of tournaments.

Carried away by his triumphs, Yvain forgets his promise and overstays the year. His wife rejects him utterly, and his grief drives him insane. Naked, starving, and amnesic, Yvain lives like an animal in the forest until he is befriended by a charitable hermit and cured of his madness by the lady of Noríson. A neighbor, Count Alier, has been attacking her property, and Yvain rallies her men and wins the war to repay her. After this victory Yvain rescues a lion from a serpent, assumes another identity, and as "the Knight with the Lion," devotes himself to the service of women in need. With the lion's help he rescues Gawain's niece and nephews from degradation or death by slaying a giant, Harpin of the Mountain, and then upon the same day rescues Lunette from death by fire by overcoming her three accusers. Disguised as "the Knight with the Lion," Yvain talks afterward with his wife and learns that the time for their reconciliation is not yet at hand.

Yvain's next triumph takes place at the Castle of Evil Adventure, where with the lion's help he rescues three hundred captive maidens by slaying two gigantic demons. He returns to King Arthur's court to defend the property rights of the younger daughter of the lord of the Black Thorn and fights incognito against Gawain, his closest friend and the best knight in the world, with whom he ties. After the battle, when his dual identity is revealed, Yvain, the Knight with the Lion, receives greater acclaim than ever before. He has also become worthy of his wife's forgiveness, which he returns to the fountain to seek, and the romance ends with their reconciliation.

Chrétien de Troyes derived the material for his romances from three sources: the British legends of King Arthur and other heroes of Celtic folklore, the French epics of Charlemagne and his knights, and the Greek and Roman myths and legends. *Yvain*'s origins are Celtic: *Yvain* is a form of *Owain*, who according to Chrétien's source commanded an army known as "The Ravens" in the sixth century, and with his father Urien, a historic king of the border district of Rheged, acquitted himself so valiantly against the Angles that King Arthur awarded him the kingdom of Scotland. Both Owain's and Urien's names were preserved in Welsh folklore. In the earlier legends Urien wooed and won the fairy of a fountain, who, with her friends, would take the form of an army of ravens to assist her son Owain in battle. As the legend was retold over the centuries, Owain supplanted his father as the wooer of "the Lady of the Fountain," whose traditional name *Laudine* is derived from the Latin name of Scotland. A shorter version of the tale of Yvain, Laudine, and the lion, "The Lady of the Fountain" was a well-established part of the repertoire of the Welsh bards (known today as *The Mabinogion*) and may have a common source with Chrétien de Troyes's romance.

Despite its traditional sources *Yvain* is not an imitation of a Celtic legend, but an original creation of the twelfth century. Yvain and his lady act in accordance with the edicts of courtly love, which were codified by Andreas Capellanus at a later date. The observations and the debates of the courts of love are interspersed throughout the romance, and a clerical antifeminism appears side by side with idealization of the lady. The romance mirrors twelfth-century society, from the sensual charm of an aristocratic house party to the miserable conditions of a silk workshop. As is often the case in medieval literature, some minor characters are presented in disproportionate detail, and many major characters are not described or named until long after they appear. The narrator is always present, commenting and forewarning, and never hesitating to interrupt the story with a discussion of love, which his listeners greatly enjoyed.

Above all, Chrétien meant to be entertaining, and the widespread popularity of his romances shows that he succeeded. His language is polished and elegant, his tone is witty, his descriptions of festivals and battles are colorful, and his debates are marvels of dialectic reasoning. He enlivens the romance with puns, proverbs, and parodies; he exaggerates and understates; he is by turns ironic and playful. His most fantastic scenes are described in meticulous detail, with distance, time, and cost carefully noted to give an aura of realism to the marvelous. The story's pace is swift, and many of the incidents are so amusingly told that at first the reader may not realize their deeper significance.

An important theme in *Yvain* is the portrayal of courtly love in marriage: an interesting idea since the prevailing opinion was that the legal obligations and enforced proximity of marriage accorded ill with a freely given, inspirational emotion, particularly one which made the lover submit to his lady's commands. Nonetheless the relationship between Yvain and his wife is one of courtly love, and their difficulties arise, not because of Yvain's pursuit of glory, but because of his broken promise to return within one year, his failure to prove a love he knew was being tested. Interpreting Yvain's forgetfulness as lack of love, the lady accordingly withdraws her own. As she will never knowingly admit Yvain to her presence again, his only hope lies in becoming a different person: establishing another identity and winning a finer reputation, which the lion helps him to do. At the end of the romance when the lady consents to see "the Knight with the Lion," Yvain has a chance to plead for forgiveness, which the lady grants to reconcile the knight and his lady as she had promised to do.

The lion however is far more than a helpful pet, and the role of the lion is one of the most disputed questions in the analysis of *Yvain*. Jean Frappier notes that in the Middle Ages the lion symbolized courage tempered by humility and, in the profane order, the perfect knight; in the spiritual order, Saviour Christ. Yvain's lion seems to fill all these roles in turn. Yvain never lacked courage, but he was indeed wanting in humility, and another theme of the romance is the rehabilitation of a knight who, at a pinnacle of worldly glory, commits the deadly sin of pride and loses what is most precious to him, the terrestial joy of his lady's love. After sinking to the level of wild beasts, mind gone, body weakened from exposure, Yvain learns humility, both from the lion's example and from sharing credit for the victories with him, as the name "the Knight with the Lion" implies. It is equally true that Yvain pursues and attains the goal of becoming a perfect knight throughout the romance and that the presence of the lion is interpreted everywhere as an indication of Yvain's worth as a knight, of his noble birth and great courage.

But at a deeper level, one of the lessons which Yvain learns is that, splendid fighter though he is, he is nothing in himself. Without the help of a charitable society he would have died insane in the forest, and without the help of God, whose aid is requested before every battle except the early ones, he would never have survived his combats with gigantic or supernatural foes. Julian Harris observes that the theory of the judicial trial by combat was that God sided with the Right, and the lion, entering the fray after Yvain, despite his best efforts, realizes that he cannot win, does seem to play the role of Christ. Together they fight increasingly dangerous battles for greater rewards; their final triumph over the demons is on a supernatural plane. Before the fight with Gawain, Yvain shows that he realizes he owes his strength and his victories to God. Without help from the lion he ties with the best knight in the world, surpasses him in courtesy, and as a perfect Christian knight, returns to his lady and is forgiven.

This translation is based upon the Guiot copy of the manuscript (Paris B.N. 794), which is available in France, Great Britain, and the United States in recently published editions. *Yvain* was translated into German verse by Hartmann von Aue at the beginning of the thirteenth century and by Ulrich Furterer at the end of the fifteenth century. There are Danish, Swedish, and Icelandic translations of the romance, and a shorter English adaption, *Ywain and Gawain*, which was prepared during the fourteenth century. Despite the great interest in medieval romances which revived in the nineteenth century, Chrétien's works were bypassed by French and English translators, for many scholars were offended by his witty and realistic treatment of love and chivalry, and by his adaption of Celtic tales to suit the themes of his romances. Chrétien's romances were edited and translated by German scholars, notably Wendelin Foerster, in the nineteenth century. Interest in Chrétien de Troyes's romances revived during the twentieth century, and their importance is widely recognized. R. W. Linker, T. B. W. Reid, and Mario Roques have edited the Guiot copy of *Yvain*, and French and English prose translations are now available.

The purpose of this verse translation is to give English-speaking readers an impression of Chrétien de Troyes as a poet as well as a storyteller. For medieval poets the form was as important as the content of their poems, and even the less exacting verse form of narrative poetry (rhymed octosyllabic couplets) influenced the poet's way of expressing his ideas. Chrétien de Troyes depended upon rhyme and meter to establish the swift pace of his romances. He used poetical images and metaphors, and frequently he employed the poetic device of rephrasing and repeating an important idea to fix it against the forward movement of the poem. These effects are lost in prose translations; worse, they seem prolix or redundant and become barriers against appreciating Chrétien's skill as a writer, which was very great. As a poet he was an innovator, responsible for making the narrative verse form more flexible by using enjambment and by breaking the couplet, for varying the traditional rhymes and assonance with identities and very rich rhymes, and for enriching and expanding the vocabulary of his time. Perhaps with a verse translation people who do not read Old French easily will be able to see Chrétien de Troyes in a different light and to appreciate his important role in the development of the Arthurian romance in French and English literature.

RUTH HARWOOD CLINE

YVAIN

OR

THE KNIGHT WITH THE LION

GOOD King Arthur of Britain, he
whose prowess taught us courtesy,
held court in Wales at Carduel,
a rich and kingly spectacle,
at that feast day of plentycost,
which we should call the Pentecost.
King Arthur's knights, when they had dined,
went into the great hall to find
the ladies and the demoiselles.
Some had the latest news to tell, 10
and others talked of Love. They told
the heartbreak and the manifold
rewards and woes that please and harry
the members of Love's monastery:
an order sweet and well endowed
to which, at present, few are vowed.
Most followers have left the place,
and Love these days is in disgrace.
The knights who loved in days of yore
were men of honor, famous for 20
their courage, courtesy, and glory.
Today Love's nothing but a story:
for men who feel no love will sigh,
say they're in love, and know they lie,
make Love a tale to tell, a cheat,
and take false pride in their deceit.
But now let's speak of those who were
and leave those men who still endure.
Far better courtly men long shrived
than crude men who are just long-lived! 30
I'm glad that I can tell a thing
or two worth hearing of a king

[1]

who was so famous that you hear
tales told about him far and near,
and I agree with Breton lore:
his name will live forevermore,
and through him people will recall
his chosen knights, the best of all,
who strove for honor, which they prized.
40 That day the courtiers were surprised
to see King Arthur rise and leave,
and many knights began to grieve
and started grumbling, commenting
that they had never seen the king
retire, at such a great feast's close,
to sleep or even seek repose.
And yet he did; the queen detained
the king, and finally he remained
with her so long that, they report,
50 he slept, and he forgot the court.

CALOGRENANT'S TALE

OUTSIDE King Arthur's bedroom door
were Didonel and Sagremore
and Kay. Also the lord Gawain
was present, and the lord Yvain,
and with them was Calogrenant,
a handsome knight and most gallant,
and he began to tell a story
more to his shame than to his glory.
But as Calogrenant related
60 his tale, the queen grew fascinated.
She rose from Arthur's side, and she
slipped out to join them quietly.

[2]

Since no one saw her by the door,
the knights stayed seated, except for
Calogrenant, who did catch sight
of her and rose to be polite.
Then Kay, who had a cutting tongue,
sarcastic, rude, abusive, flung
at him, "My God, Calogrenant,
aren't you outstandingly gallant!   70
Why, how delightful to recall
that you're most chivalrous of all!
I'm sure that you believe it too,
you lily-livered creature, you!
How right Her Majesty should see
that you are better bred than we:
we're just too lazy, I expect,
or did not rise from disrespect!
My God, sir, let me tell you, we
sat still because we didn't see   80
my lady; you did and you stood!"

"Kay, you'd explode, I know you would,
You'd simply burst," replied the queen,
"if you could never vent the spleen
that fills you full! Kay, you offend
us all by fighting with your friend."

"My lady, if we haven't gained
because you're with us," Kay complained,
"at least take care that we don't lose.
No words of mine need an excuse!   90
Please say no more, put it aside.
There is no courtesy or pride
in keeping up a quarrel. Friend,
I think our argument should end
before it starts to gain in price!

[3]

Let him begin again and splice
it on the story he began;
then we won't have to scold the man."
"My lady," Calogrenant replied,
"Kay's scolding hasn't hurt my pride;
his insults have small worth and measure.
If I've incurred Sir Kay's displeasure,
it doesn't make me worry. Why,
to better, wiser men than I,
I've often overheard, Sir Kay,
the vile, insulting things you say!
It's just a habit, and I think,
that as manure will always stink,
and bees will buzz, and horseflies sting,
a mean man keeps on slandering.
But I'll relate no more today,
if you will let me have my way.
I beg you, lady, let me be!
The story now displeases me;
don't make me tell it; please be kind."

"My lady," Kay said, "you will find
that every man here, without fail,
will thank you if we hear the tale.
I wouldn't ask for anything,
but by the faith you owe the king,
your lord and my lord, bid him tell
his story now. You would do well."
The queen replied, "Calogrenant,
pay no attention to the taunt
of my lord Kay the seneschal.
He likes to slander one and all,
and no one can correct him for it,
so I command you to ignore it.

[4]

Please keep no anger in your heart
against Sir Kay, but rather, start   130
a story we would like to hear.
If you wish me to hold you dear,
then start to tell the tale again."

"My lady, it will cause me pain
to do as you command me. I
would much prefer to lose an eye
than to continue with my tale.
But your displeasure makes me quail,
so I will do as you request
and suffer pain to please you best.   140
Now listen! and before I start,
give me your hearing and your heart,
for words will quickly disappear,
if they aren't heard in heart *and* ear.
Some men will hear and then commend
things that they cannot comprehend.
Their sense of hearing lets them hear it,
but once the heart has lost the spirit,
the words will fall upon the ears
just like the wind that blows and veers.   150
The words don't linger there or stay;
in a short while they fly away,
if the unwary heart's asleep,
because the heart alone can keep
the words enclosed. The ears, they say,
are just the channel and the way
by which the voice comes to the heart.
But the heart's able to impart
the voice that enters through the ears
unto the breast of him who hears.   160
So he who would hear me must start

[5]

by giving me his ears and heart,
because, however it may seem,
it's not a lie, tall tale, or dream."

Once, seven long years from the present,
as solitary as a peasant,
I had gone off adventuring.
My armor shone. I'd thought to bring
all weapons proper for a knight.

170   The path I took turned to the right
within a forest thick and deep.
The path was treacherous and steep
obscured by clumps of thorn and briar.
Despite discomfort, the entire
day long I followed it till I'd
come out upon the other side
of the wood called Brocéliande.
Beyond the trees, in open land,
I saw a tower on my way.

180   One half a Welsh league off it lay;
perhaps that far off, but no more,
so I rode toward it to explore.
I reached the tower. On each side
there was a moat, long, deep, and wide,
and on the bridge a gentleman,
a molted falcon on his hand,
who almost asked me to alight
before I'd hailed him. The polite
good gentleman came toward me, and

190   he held my stirrup in his hand.
So I got down without protesting;
indeed I felt in need of resting.
The road that led me to his door
he blessed one hundred times and more.
We crossed the drawbridge and went straight

into the courtyard through the gate.
Within the courtyard of the lord
(such joy and honor God accord
to him as he gave me that day!)
there hung a gong, which I would say   200
was not of iron, or of wood,
but of pure copper, fine and good.
A hammer hung beside the gong.
He struck it three times, loud and strong,
and everybody that was in
the house could hear the noise and din,
and gathered in the court with speed.
As I dismounted from my steed,
which one of the attendants led
away, I saw a fair, well-bred,   210
tall, slim maid come to welcome me.
She greeted me and expertly
removed my armor while she spoke.
She dressed me in a short silk cloak
of peacock blue and lined with vair.
The other people left us there.
No one remained, which suited me;
she was the one I wished to see!
The maid took me to sit and rest
in a small court, the prettiest   220
in all the world. There was a wall
around the courtyard, low and small.
I found the maid so very charming,
so wise, well spoken, and disarming,
of such fine mien and character,
it was a joy to be with her.
I didn't want to move away,
however at the close of day
I had to do so all the same,
for at that hour my good host came   230

[7]

to tell me it was time we dined.
Of course I could not stay behind,
so I complied with his request
and went to supper as his guest.
But it was settled perfectly:
the maiden sat across from me.
When we had finished, my host sighed
and said that he could not decide
how long a space of time had passed
240   since errant knights had lodged there last,
though many'd come adventuring
in days gone by. He asked one thing,
would I stay there another day?
I promised to come back that way.
An easy wish to gratify,
and how disgraceful to deny
a favor of the uttermost
simplicity to a kind host!

"Well lodged indeed was I that night.
250   Soon as I saw the morning light,
my horse was saddled, at the door,
as I had asked the night before.
Then I commended the good host
and daughter to the Holy Ghost.
I took my leave, and I went on
soon after, but I had not gone
far from the good host's courtyard when
I found bulls fighting in a glen.
The wild bulls made a noise so great
260   and terrible, that I must state
I drew back. It's excusable!
No beast is fiercer than a bull;
no animal's as quick to gore.
A creature who looked like a Moor,

and was so ugly, and so black,
and hideous, I find I lack
words to describe him fully, sat
upon a stump. I noticed that
he held a huge club in his hand.
I drew close to the creature, and   270
I saw his head's size was enormous,
a huger head than any horse's
or other beast's, with tufts of hair.
His forehead was completely bare
and measured more than two spans wide.
The creature's head had on each side
a huge ear filled with mossy plants,
just like the ears of elephants.
His brows were full, his face was flat,
with owlish eyes, the nose of a cat.   280
His wolfish mouth was split apart
by wild boar's teeth, bloodred and sharp.
His head was red; his whiskers tangled;
his chin against his chest was angled.
His long spine twisted in a hump.
The creature sat upon the stump
and leaned upon his club. He wore
no wool or linen clothing, for
instead, the fellow was arrayed
in two wild bulls' hides, newly flayed
and hung around his neck. The boor — *LOWER CLASS PERSON* 290
stood when he saw me. I made sure,
although I didn't know exactly
what he would do, perhaps attack me,
that I was ready for him, till
I noticed he was standing still.
He leaned against a fallen tree,
and then I realized that he
was seventeen feet tall, at least.

[9]

300 He said no more than any beast
would say, but watched me, and I thought,
perhaps the fellow couldn't talk
or had no wits. I thought I would
speak boldly. 'Now, are you a good
or evil thing? Speak if you can!'
And he replied, 'I am a man.'
'What kind of man?' 'Such as you find.
I've never been another kind.'
'What do you do, then?' 'Here I stand
310 and tend bulls in this wood and land.'
'You tend them? By Saint Peter of Rome,
what human hand could they have known?
I don't think anybody could
tend such wild beasts in meadow, wood,
or any place that can be found,
if they are not enclosed or bound.'
'I tend these bulls and do such good
work that they never leave the wood.'
'How do you do it?' 'There's not one
320 who'd dare move when he sees me come.
When I catch one, I wrench his horns
so hard with my two fists, it warns
the others. They come trembling, scared,
and start to beg me to be spared.
The people here so greatly fear them,
no one but me would dare come near them;
if someone did, I'm sure the lot
of bulls would kill him on the spot.
So I am master of my herd,
330 and now I think it's time I heard
what man you are and what you want.'
I said, 'I am a knight-errant
who seeks what he cannot obtain.
Long have I searched and searched in vain.'

[10]

'What do you seek?' 'Adventure, so
I'll test my courage, and I'll show
my prowess. Please, what do you hear
of marvels and adventures here?'
He said, 'You'll have to do without
those things. I've never heard about   340
adventures here, and I don't know
what marvels are, but if you go
not far off to a little spring,
you won't leave without suffering
much pain, if you observe the rite.
Close by here, over on the right,
is a small path that leads you there.
Be sure to follow it with care.
Go straight ahead, and do not stray
on other paths that cross your way.   350
Soon you will see a bubbling spring
with stone-cold water, nestling
within the shade of the most fair
tree Nature formed. Its branches bear
green leaves the year around and hold
their leaves fast even in the cold.
An iron basin hangs suspended
on a long chain that, when extended,
will reach the fountain, where you'll find
a great stone. I don't know what kind   360
of stone it is: I must admit
I've never seen a stone like it.
There is a chapel by the spring;
it is a very pretty thing.
Just pick the basin up and spill
some water on the stone: you will
start such an awful storm that way,
no animal would dare to stay
in Brocéliande. At once the deer,

[11]

370 wild boars, and birds will disappear,
for you will see the lightning flash,
the wind blow till the tall trees crash
around you, thunderbolts, and rain.
If you escape without much pain,
you will have had great luck, far more
than any knight who came before.'

"Toward noon I left the herdsman when
he'd pointed out the right path. Then,
soon after midday I could see
380 the fountain underneath the tree.
The tree must be a pine, I knew,
the loveliest that ever grew,
with boughs so thick, it seemed to me
no waterdrop could wet the tree
in hardest rainfalls; rain would slide
right off the branches. Then I spied
a basin on the tree, of gold,
the finest that was ever sold
in any fair. The spring did seem
390 to boil. An emerald, bright green,
shaped like a sieve, was the great stone,
with small holes on a ruby throne.
Beneath the emerald were four
bright rubies, blazing red and more
aflame with color than the sun
at morning in the east. Now none
of this is false! I wished to see
the marvel: how the spring and tree
provoked the storms. I realize
400 today I was not very wise.
I so regretted my rash act,
I'd have undone the deed, in fact,

one moment after I had filled
the basin to the brim and spilled
the water on the stone. Deploring
how much spring water I'd been pouring,
in fourteen spots I saw the skies
split open, dazzling my eyes.
From clouds piled high on clouds there fell
snow mixed with rain, and hail as well.   410
So violent were the wind and rain,
that I was very nearly slain
by lightning striking all around
and crashing trees split to the ground.
Believe me, I was much afraid
until the violent storm was stayed,
but God soon gave me reassurance
it would not be of long endurance.
In a short while the winds grew slow,
and when God pleased, they dared not blow.   420
Once I could see the clear, pure air,
I felt great joy, beyond compare,
for joy, as I learned long ago,
makes one forget the greatest woe.
Once that the thunderstorm had passed,
upon the pine I saw birds massed
so thickly—it's beyond belief—
that I could see no branch or leaf.
The tree was hidden, but more fair,
because the birds were perching there.   430
They sang one sweet song in the tree,
and then they sang in harmony.
Each bird knew different songs. I heard
no bird sing like another bird.
Each bird knew many melodies.
I listened to their harmonies

with greatest joy, while in the pine
the birds sang services divine,
for I had never, till that time,
440   heard such tremendous joy, and I'm
sure no man has or will, till he
has come and heard this melody.
It brought me joy and so enhanced
my rapture, like a fool, entranced,
I waited there until I heard
knights galloping. I thought there were
at least ten, judging by the sound.
But all the noise and din, I found,
were caused by one knight. Then, of course,
450   I went at once to catch my horse
and mounted quickly. I could see
the great knight riding up to me,
aflame with anger, full of evil
intentions, swifter than an eagle,
as fierce as any lion living.
When I could hear, he started giving
his challenge:
           " 'Without provocation
you brought about this devastation,
vassal, to cause me harm and shame!
460   If you were fair, you would proclaim
your challenge, if you've grievance, or
seek justice first and then wage war!
Sir vassal, if I can, I will
repay you for your terrible,
outrageous acts of violence!
Around me is the evidence
of harm you've done to my domain.
He who is injured may complain,
and I say you've no right to chase

[14]

a man from his own dwelling place 470
with thunderbolts and wind and rain!
You've caused me great distress and pain,
and cursed be he who thinks it good!
Upon my word and town and wood,
you have attacked me so directly,
that men-at-arms could not protect me,
nor could strong towers and high walls.
No one could feel safe in these squalls,
not even if, by luck, he stood
within a fort of stone and wood! 480
I tell you, vassal, it's no use
to ask for peace or any truce!'

"And then we rode against each other
and held our shields so they would cover
our bodies. But his lance indeed
was stout; he had a splendid steed.
He was a big man, a head taller
than I am, and my horse was smaller
than his horse, so I think it apt
to say that I was handicapped. 490
I hope these factors will efface
part of the shame of my disgrace.
The hardest blow that I could wield
I landed squarely on his shield,
and I'd put all my strength in it.
His lance stayed whole, while mine was split
and shattered, for it was not light.
No other lance I've seen a knight
bear weighed as much. It must have been
the thickest lance I've seen. And then 500
the knight rode toward me to attack
with such a blow, he knocked me back

[15]

over my horse's crop, and set me
down flat upon the ground, and let me
lie there, worn out and filled with shame.
He never looked at me. He came
and simply took my horse's rein
and rode off up the path again.
I couldn't think what to do next.
510   I lay there hurt and greatly vexed.
I spent some time there gathering
my thoughts, and sat beside the spring.
I didn't dare pursue the knight,
because I was afraid I might
do something rash. In any event
I didn't know which way he went.
A short time later I began
to think I'd told the gentleman
that I would lodge with him that night.
520   The idea caused me much delight.
But first I needed to remove
my armor, so that I could move
more easily. Then I retraced
my steps back to his house, disgraced.
I found my host was as polite
and gracious as he'd been the night
before. His daughter dear and he
received me just as courteously,
and showed me as much kindliness
530   and honor as before, no less.
I'm very grateful for the way
they treated me throughout my stay.
But all the other knights, they said,
were either prisoners or dead,
who went from where I had returned,
according to what news they'd learned.
And so I went, and so I came,

[16]

and called myself a fool by name,
and foolishly I've told you all.
I didn't want to tell at all!"   540

"Calogrenant!" said Sir Yvain,
"you're my first cousin, and it's plain
that we should love each other dearly.
And yet you were a fool most clearly
to have concealed this tale from me!
If I have called you fool, don't be
offended by my admonition,
for, if I can and have permission,
I will avenge your shame, I vow."

PRIDE TO TRY TO GET THE GLORY

Kay cried, "It's after dinner now!"   550
He had to speak! "There are more fine
words swimming in a pot of wine
than in a barrel full of beer!
They say drunk cats are full of cheer!
When dinner's over, men sit back
and boast they're ready to attack
Forré and see Noradin killed!
Your saddlebags, sir, are they filled?
Your armor's shined for this campaign?
Your flag's unfurled, my lord Yvain?   560
Please tell me quickly, in God's sight,
do you leave tomorrow or tonight?
Be sure to let us know afar, sir,
when you are going to be a martyr,
for every provost and sheriff's man
will go there with you if he can,
and we will keep you company!
So please, however it may be,
on no account, no matter why,
don't leave us till you've said good-bye!   570

[17]

And if, tonight, you have bad dreams,
why, stay at home, forget your schemes!"

"Are you beside yourself, Sir Kay,
to let your tongue run on this way?
Cursed be the tongue," exclaimed the queen,
"that is so bitter, full of spleen!
I'm sure your tongue must hate you, so
it says the worst things it may know
to everybody, as it pleases!
580   Cursed be a tongue that never ceases
to speak vile words! It runs away
till all men hate you. To betray
you purposely, your tongue could find
nothing worse to do. If it were mine,
I'd have it brought to trial for treason.
Just as a man who's lost his reason
is brought to church, and once inside,
before the chancel gate is tied,
a man who cannot be corrected
590   deserves full well to be subjected
to the same kind of punishment!"

Said Sir Yvain, "Kay's insolent,
and yet it doesn't bother me.
Sir Kay has such ability,
such wisdom and such great aplomb,
he never will be deaf or dumb
in any court. When offered low,
ill-mannered speech, he'll always know
some thoughtful, courteous reply.
600   Now you would all know if I lie!
We've had one foolish quarrel today,
so I don't want to fight with Kay.
They say the man who starts the fight

is not the man who chose to light
the first blow: no, the man he hit
begins the fight avenging it,
and he who fights with friends would be
more wise to fight an enemy.
I don't want to seem like the cur
that bares his teeth and lifts his fur   610
at other dogs that bark and snarl."

The king came in to end the quarrel.
He left his bedroom, where he'd kept
far from his guests and overslept,
and all the barons there, to greet
the king, sprang quickly to their feet.
King Arthur told them to be seated.
He sat down, and the queen repeated
Calogrenant's tale, word for word,
with all the details they had heard.   620
She told it sweetly and with skill.
King Arthur listened with a will.
Then he arose, and there before
the barons, three great oaths he swore:
by the souls of Uther Pendragon,
and of King Arthur's mother and son,
he'd travel to Brocéliande
to see the magic fountain and
the storm within two weeks at least.
Before Saint John the Baptist's feast,   630
he'd be there, and he'd spend the night,
and everyone who wished to might
accompany him. The whole court found
the king's plan excellent and sound,
and every baron, youth, and knight
thought of the journey with delight.

[19]

BUT while the courtiers were so glad,
the lord Yvain was very sad
and much displeased, for he had planned
640   to journey to Brocéliande
alone, and now King Arthur thought
he'd travel there with all his court.
The lord Yvain knew Kay would fight
beside the fountain with the knight.
Most surely, if Sir Kay should choose
to fight, the king would not refuse.
Or else, perhaps the lord Gawain
would ask to fight first: Sir Yvain
could not fight if one of these two
650   asked first, as they would surely do.
He did not want their company
and would not wait for them, but he
would travel by himself and go
to seek great joy or greater woe.
Another man might have preferred
to stay at court, but on the third
day he would reach Brocéliande wood,
where he would search until he could
find all the marvels he desires:
660   the narrow pathway filled with briars,
the open plain, the tower, the aid
and welcome of the lovely maid,
who was so charming and so bright,
so beautiful and so polite,
and the good host, who did his best
to lodge and honor every guest.
He'd see the wild bulls in the glen;
the giant herdsman tending them.

Indeed, he'd like to see him with
his body black as any smith   670
and such a twisted back, who'd shown
his cousin to the great green stone,
gold basin, and the magic spring,
and in the pine, birds caroling.
Then he would start the wind and rain!
He would not boast of this again,
and he'd make certain no one knew
about his plans till he was through
and greatly honored or ashamed.
Then let the true facts be proclaimed!   680

Alone the lord Yvain withdrew,
avoiding everyone he knew.
He left the court behind and then
went to his house and called his men,
told them to saddle up his steed,
and called a trusted squire. "I need
my armor. Keep it secret, for
when I go out through the main door,
I'm going to ride my palfrey. Pray
make certain there is no delay;   690
the trip I'm taking will be long.
Shoe my war horse, bring him along,
then lead the palfrey back again.
I order you," said Sir Yvain,
"if anybody asks for me,
say nothing, for I guarantee
that you can count on me, but give
out news of me, and while you live,
you won't count on me anymore!"

The squire said, "Please be calm, my lord.   700
I promise you no one will know

about your plans from me. Now go
and I will follow." Sir Yvain
rode off; he hoped his cousin's shame
would be avenged by some great deed
before he came back. On the steed
the squire followed. He didn't lose
a moment, since the horse's shoes
were new and didn't need fresh nails.

710 He rode along his master's trails
and saw him standing in a cleared
spot, waiting till the squire appeared.
The squire brought armor, bit, and rein,
and armed and dressed the lord Yvain.
Then Sir Yvain did not delay;
once he was armed he made his way
down valley and up mountainside,
on into forests deep and wide.
He went through many wicked passes,

720 through many treacherous, wild morasses
and eerie places, and rode all day
until he saw the narrow way.
The thorns and briars made it obscure.
At that point Sir Yvain felt sure
there was no chance he'd lose his way.
Whatever price he'd have to pay,
he would not stop until he'd seen,
overshadowed by the evergreen,
the fountain, great stone, and the gale

730 with thunderbolts, wind, rain, and hail.

That night his lodgings pleased him well.
He found the lovely demoiselle
one hundred times more wise and fair
than he had heard told anywhere.
The welcome of the gentleman

[22]

was far more kind and gracious than
I could find time to tell you. Some
say you can never tell the sum
of all the qualities you find
in men and women good and kind.   740
The count will never be complete,
because the tongue cannot repeat
all noble deeds an honest man
could carry out in his life's span.
And so the lord Yvain that night
was well lodged, much to his delight.
Next day he came into the glen
and found the bulls and herdsman. Then,
you may be sure, one hundred times
or more, the lord Yvain made signs   750
of the cross, because he was aghast
that Nature knew a way to cast
so rough and hideous a thing.
He went ahead and reached the spring,
which he so wished to see. The lord
did not sit down or pause; he poured
some water on the great green stone.
The storm came, just as he had known
it would, with gales of wind and rain.
When God gave sunshine once again,   760
the birds came to the pine to sing
with joy above the parlous spring.

THE STORM KNIGHT

BEFORE they stopped, a warrior came.
The knight burned like a log aflame
with anger, and he yelled as much

as if he chased a stag in rut.
The two knights faced each other, rode
together, and each warrior showed
the other knight with gestures grim
770   how mortally he hated him.
Each had a stiff, strong lance to wield
hard blows, and each knight pierced the shield
at his foe's neck, cut his mail, vying
to break his lance, with splinters flying
into the air! The knights attacked
each other with their swords, and hacked
apart the straps each used to seize his
broad shield, and cut the shield to pieces.
The shields were split from end to end
780   and far too shattered to defend
the knights. With bright swords, they applied
hard blows to rib, arm, flank, and side.
They fought with murderous dispositions
and moved no more from their positions
than two stones. There were never two
brave warriors more determined to
cut short their lives. They did not spare
their blows; they landed each one where
it would hurt most. Their helmets bent,
790   and meshes from their hauberks went
through the air, and much blood flowed, since
their bodies' heat was so intense,
their hauberks gave them even less
protection than the knights' cloth dress.
They slashed their faces. I'm aghast!
How long can such a battle last?
Both warriors were of such worth
that neither'd yield a foot of earth
until he'd struck a deadly blow.
800   Yet they were men of honor, so

[24]

that neither of the knights used force
to try to strike or harm a horse
throughout their battle, so the fight
was elegant, because each knight
stayed seated on his war horse and
did not set foot upon the land.

But finally the lord Yvain
crushed the knight's helmet flat. The pain
of the blow Sir Yvain had dealt
made him grow faint. He'd never felt   810
in all his life a blow so dread.
Beneath his cloth head cap, his head
was split wide open to the brain.
The brains and blood began to stain
his hauberk's mesh of shining mail.
The knight, in agony, death-pale,
his heart about to cease to beat,
turned round and fled in his defeat,
and he acquired no shame thereby.
He knew that he was going to die;   820
he could not strike the warrior down;
and so he galloped toward his town.
The bridge was lowered, and inside
the entrance gate was opened wide.
The lord Yvain spurred on his steed
and followed him at topmost speed.
The knight fled, and the lord Yvain—
as the gyrfalcon hunts the crane
he's sighted rising far away,
and flies so close beside his prey,   830
he's certain he's about to clutch her,
and yet he cannot even touch her—
was like the falcon, for he chased him
so closely he almost embraced him,

but could not quite come alongside.
So close behind him did he ride,
he heard the warrior groan in pain.
The knight rode on; the lord Yvain
kept up and would not be outpaced.
840   He thought his efforts were a waste
if, dead or alive, he hadn't caught
the knight, for Sir Yvain still thought
about the insults Kay'd alleged.
He had not done the deed he'd pledged
his cousin, and he knew no one
would ever credit what he'd done,
unless he brought back proof. The two
knights spurred their horses and rode through
the outer gate and castle wall.
850   In town they found no one at all:
the streets were bare. At the same rate
of speed, they reached the palace gate.

The gate itself was high and wide,
but narrow was the way inside.
Two knights on horseback, they attest,
could not pass through the gate abreast
without great difficulty, for
the sliding gate that formed the door
was like a rat trap which is made
860   to kill rats with a hanging blade,
which suddenly can be released
to fall and strike and catch the beast
that brushed against the spring. It seems,
beneath the gate, two slender beams
propped up the door, one on each side.
The iron gate was sharp and wide.
If anybody touched the spring,
the great door fell on anything

proceeding through the gate below.
The road beneath the door was no 870
wider than a path would be.
The wounded knight, deliberately,
rode straight through, and the lord Yvain
raced after, managing to gain
so much ground that he'd gotten so
close that he held the saddle bow.
The lord Yvain was lucky he'd
stretched so far forward on his steed,
because he'd have been cut in two
when his horse brushed the beam joined to 880
the gate, were he not placed so well.
The great door, like a fiend from Hell,
crashed down and cut his horse in twain,
and yet the valiant lord Yvain
was scarcely touched, may God be praised!
excepting that his back was grazed
by the iron door, and he could feel
his spurs were sliced off at the heel.
As he collapsed in great dismay,
the knight eluded him this way: 890
there was another door ahead
like that behind him; the knight fled
out of the hallway through that door,
which dropped down like the one before.
And so the lord Yvain was caught!
He was distressed and overwrought
at being shut inside the hall.
The roof had golden nails; each wall
displayed rare paints used skillfully.
Not knowing where the knight might be 900
grieved Sir Yvain the most of all.
While he was standing in the hall,
he heard a small door open wide

out of a little room beside
the hallway, and he saw a fair
and charming maiden standing there.
She'd turned to close the door again.
But when she saw the lord Yvain,
at first the maid was seized by fright.

910 She said to him, "Indeed, Sir knight,
you are ill-come, or so I fear!
If anybody finds you here,
you'll be mincemeat! My lord is lying
inside upon his bed and dying
of mortal wounds, sir, and I know
you murdered him. My lady's so
undone by grief, and all her men
are in such uproar, they have been
half killed by sorrow. They can guess
920 you're in here now, but their distress
is so great, they can't deal with you.
Once they've decided what to do,
behead or hang you, I know they'll
come here to find you and won't fail
to keep their plans to have you slain!"

"Please God," replied the lord Yvain,
"I won't be slaughtered by her men
or taken prisoner by them."

"No," she replied, "for I will do
930 all that I can to rescue you.
No real man is too much afraid,
and since you are not too dismayed,
I think you are a valiant man
whom I will help as best I can,
because one time you did the same

[28]

for me at Arthur's court. I came
to bring a message; I surmise
I wasn't well behaved, and wise,
and courteous as a maid should be.
No knight would speak one word to me,   940
except for you! You were so kind
and waited on me. You will find
that I will give you your reward
for honoring me then, my lord,
and I remember you by name.
I know you are the lord Yvain;
your father is King Urien.
My lord, if you will trust me, then
there is no need to be alarmed;
you won't be captured or be harmed.   950
Take my ring: give it back to me,
please, only when I've set you free."

The maid gave him the ring to wear
and said its power she could compare
to bark that grows upon a tree
and covers it: no one can see
the wood beneath. Put the ring on,
then turn the stone in toward your palm,
and you need not fear anything,
for anyone who wears the ring   960
upon his finger can't be seen
by any man, however keen
his eyes, just as you cannot see
the wood when bark grows on the tree.
The lord Yvain was highly pleased,
and when the maiden's words had ceased,
she had him sit upon a bed.
Its quilt was such a costly spread,
the duke of Austria owned no thing

[29]

970
as valuable. She said she'd bring
food if he cared to eat. He said
he did, and so the maiden sped
back to the room and brought a fine
roast capon and a pot of wine
of a good vintage, in a neat
white napkin for her guest to eat.
She brought this meal to Sir Yvain
and tried to serve and entertain
her guest. As he felt starved, he ate,
980
and drank, and did not hesitate!

The knights began to try to find
the lord Yvain, when he had dined,
to mete out punishment severe;
their lord lay dead upon his bier.
"The lady's liege men, as I knew,
are coming here to look for you.
What great commotion! What a din!
No matter who goes out or in,
you never will be found," she said,
990
"if you do not move from this bed.
The hall will fill with troublesome,
revengeful people, who will come
and feel sure of discovering
that you're in here. I think they'll bring
the body through for burial.
Then I am certain, one and all,
they'll seek you under bench and chair.
But for a man who doesn't scare,
I think it will be fun to find
1000
a room of people who are blind.
You'll find the magic ring won't let them
see you in here, which will upset them
and make them angry. I can't say

[30]

more now, because I dare not stay.
I thank God He has given me
the chance and the ability
to do something that pleases you,
which I had greatly wished to do."
The maiden left the hallway. When
she'd gone, all of the lady's men   1010
ran up from both sides to the gate
with swords and clubs. Their rage was great,
exactly as the maid had said.
When these cruel men saw half the dead
horse lying at the main gate, cleaved
in two, they certainly believed
that when the door was raised, they'd fall
upon their victim in the hall.
The liege men had the door raised high:
it had made many warriors die,   1020
but since no one had set the spring,
they entered without worrying.
The other part of the dead horse
was all they found. No eyes, of course,
could ever see the lord Yvain,
whom they would willingly have slain,
and he could see their anger grow.
They started shouting, "Where'd he go?
There's no way any man could try
to get out, if he couldn't fly,   1030
for only squirrels, or field rats, or
small animals slip through the door!
See how the window bars are fast.
The moment that our lord went past,
we dropped the sliding doors. It's clear,
alive or dead, he must be here,
because he cannot be outside!
His saddle's in here, but we've spied

[31]

no traces of the killer but
1040 these spurs that fell from his feet, cut
off by the iron door! Start poking
in every corner! Now, no joking!
We know the warrior has to be
in here, or else by treachery
we must have been bewitched today,
or demons stole the man away!"
Aflame with rage, the liege men all
looked for their man within the hall.
They beat the benches, walls, and bed,
1050 but they did not strike at the spread
upon the couch where Sir Yvain
was lying; he did not sustain
one blow then. But the liege men soon
raised such an uproar in the room,
they used their clubs like blind men, tapping
and pounding on the beds, and rapping
beneath the stools, and then began
a second search to find their man!

THE LADY OF LANDUC

THEN the most beautiful of all
1060 terrestial ladies reached the hall.
No Christian lady ever told
was half so lovely to behold,
but she was utterly beside
herself and close to suicide.
The lady screamed without restraint,
and then fell backward in a faint.
The others helped her. She arose,
and in a frenzy tore her clothes,

[32]

and clawed herself, and pulled out strands
of hair, and wept, and wrung her hands. 1070
At every step she swooned again,
for nobody could ease her pain
when she had seen her husband dead
upon the bier, borne out ahead.
The widow cried out, uncontrolled,
and thought she'd never be consoled.
The ladies of a convent bore
the cross and water on before.
The priests brought candles, and the censers,
and missals, being the dispensers 1080
of absolution, which would free
the wretched soul from misery.

The lord Yvain heard her distress
and cries, which words cannot express,
because nobody ever took
such grief and wrote it in a book.
Then the procession passed him by.
Within the hall there rose a cry!
Everyone crowded around the bier.
Warm, red blood started to appear 1090
and trickle from the dead man's wounds.
The blood proved what they had assumed:
the man was present who'd surpassed
their lord in battle and at last
had killed him. Then the men looked through
the hall again and searched anew,
till everyone was drenched with sweat,
for they were terribly upset
to see the red blood start to flow.
The lord Yvain took many a blow, 1100
but did not move from where he lay.
Then the men shouted with dismay,

because the wounds burst open wide
upon a corpse. The liege men tried
to reason why the red blood ran.
They could not find the guilty man,
and made tremendous noise and fuss.
"The murderer's in here with us,
and yet we cannot see him here!

1110   It's magic, Satan's work, that's clear!"

The lady had grown so beside
herself with sorrow that she cried
as if insane, "God! Won't we find
the wicked man who killed my kind
good husband? Good? Why, certainly
the best of men! The fault will be
yours solely, God, if he gets out.
I'll blame You for it! There's no doubt
we've never seen such power before,

1120   and nobody has wronged me more
than You have, not to let me see
a man who must be close to me!
I think, because I see no one,
some devil or some phantom's come
among us, or perhaps I fell
beneath some sort of magic spell,
or he's a coward, scared of me!
Why, what a coward he must be
to fear me! So it's cowardice

1130   that makes him hide from me like this!
Oh, phantom! What a cowardly thing!
Why fear me now, considering
how brave you were with my lord, and
why can't I have you in my hand?
Why won't your magic powers dim?
Why can't I touch you? You tricked him!

[34]

Except by treachery abhorred,
how could you ever kill my lord?
I know my lord would not have been
killed if he'd seen you. God and men   1140
knew of no man that was his peer
on earth, nor know one now! It's clear
my lord's slain by some apparition!
He had no human competition!"

Accordingly the lady fought,
till she was tired and overwrought
from struggling with herself. She went
out with her household to lament.
The liege men took the corpse away
and buried it. They'd searched all day   1150
and finally stopped exhausted, for
they found no one inside the door
whom they suspected of the crime.
The priests and nuns had, by this time,
finished the funeral service. All
went from church to the burial.
The maid within the room was not
concerned with them. She only thought
the more about the lord Yvain.
Soon she went in to him again   1160
and said to him, "My lord, I fear
there was a crowd of people here.
They checked each place, and stormed around,
and searched more carefully than a hound
would search for partridges or quail.
You must have been scared, without fail!"
"My word, I was quite truthfully
more frightened than I thought I'd be!
But still, I wish that I could stand
beside some door or window, and   1170

[35]

I'd like to look outside and hear
the people march by with the bier."

But he did not intend to watch
the dead man and the funeral march:
he wished they'd all go up in sparks,
if it cost him one hundred marks!
One hundred marks? Why, it would be
one hundred thousand marks! But he
would see the lady of the town.

1180   The maid had Sir Yvain sit down
beside a window. Each request
she granted, and she did her best
to be as courteous as we know
he'd been to her so long ago.
The lord could see the beautiful
lady saying, "God be merciful
to your soul, dearest husband, for
I know no other warrior
that ever rode on horseback, who

1190   in any way could equal you.
No other knight, my dear, fair lord,
was so admired and so adored,
or worthy of your company.
You showed such generosity,
and courage was your closest friend.
I pray that the Lord God will send
your soul among the saints to dwell!"
The lady struck, and tore, and fell
on all she could reach. Sir Yvain

1200   could hardly manage to restrain
himself from running to her and
endeavoring to seize her hand.
The maiden stopped him, and commanded,
and begged, and warned, and reprimanded

[36]

him graciously. She used her tact
and told him gently not to act
so foolishly. "My lord Yvain,
you are well off here. Please remain,
and do not move from where you're hidden
until she's dried her tears and bidden   1210
her liege men to depart. They'll leave
at once, and she'll stay here to grieve.
If you will do as I think best
and carry out what I request,
you've much to gain. Sit here, and stay,
and watch the men go on their way
indoors and out. Since no one can
see you, you know you have quite an
advantage. Don't speak recklessly.
Who, at each opportunity,   1220
becomes upset, and starts to scold
and clench his fist in rage, I hold
a man more rash than brave. Take care,
if some wild thought comes, and forbear
to act on it. The prudent man
uses as much sense as he can,
and hides his foolish thoughts. Be wise,
act sensibly, as I advise.
Don't risk your head, for which they'd take
no ransom, and for your own sake,   1230
don't move from here till I return.
I can't stay longer, lest they learn
I was not with them in the throng.
If I stay here with you too long,
I'll be severely criticized."

The maiden left. He stayed, disguised
and wondering how he should behave.
The corpse was buried in the grave,

and he was most unhappy, since
1240   he had no proof or evidence
that he had killed the knight to bring
to show the council and the king.
Without some way to prove his claim,
he knew he would be brought to shame,
because Sir Kay took such delight
in malice, ridicule, and spite,
he'd not believe the lord Yvain.
Kay would start taunting him again
and find insulting things to say,
1250   the way he'd done the other day.
Still fresh and rankling, the smart
of Kay's words burned within his heart.
But now, a new Love sweetens him
with sugar and honey. Love, at whim,
has hunted in her lands today,
and now she gathers in her prey.
His enemy has his heart. He'll love
the one who hates him far above
all other men on earth, so she
1260   avenged her lord unknowingly,
and Love's revenge will soon have grown
worse than she could have done alone,
since Love's pursuit's a gentle art:
through the knight's eyes she strikes his heart.
The wound that Love has dealt the lord
won't heal like wounds from lance or sword,
for any wound a sword has cut
the doctors can cure quickly, but
the wounds of Love, by definition,
1270   are worst when nearest their physician.

So wounded is the lord Yvain,
and he will not be whole again,

[38]

since Love's possessed him totally
and left the place she used to be.
She wants no other house or host
but him, and she is being most
well-bred to leave a place profane
and give herself to Sir Yvain.
She doesn't want to live elsewhere.
At times her lodgings don't compare   1280
with this one! It has caused dismay
that Love so often acts this way:
that sometimes she can be so base,
and dwell in the worst lodging place
that she can find as willingly
as in the best place. But now she
is welcome; she'll be well received,
and certainly will not be grieved
by her new lodgings and her stay.
Love really should behave this way,   1290
for she is such a noble thing,
that it's a wonder she can bring
herself to lodge in dirt and shame.
Though some hate honor, and love blame,
and spread their balm on ash and soil,
put soot in honey, and would spoil
sweet sugar, mixing it with gall,
Love should not act this way at all!
But this time Love has not been base;
she's lodged in such a noble place,   1300
no one can say one chiding word.

When the dead man had been interred,
the lady's household went away.
No servants and no clerks would stay,
nor knights and ladies, only she
who could not hide her agony

[39]

stayed in the palace all alone.
She clutched her throat, began to moan
and wring her hands, and beat her palms,
1310 and in her psalter read her psalms.
Its letters were illuminated
in gold. The lord Yvain still waited
beside the window, and the lord
thought her more lovely and adored
her more, the more he saw her. Why,
he wished she'd cease to weep and cry,
and that she would consent to talk
with him! So it was Love who caught
him at the window to inspire
1320 and fill him with this great desire.
He thought his prayers would not be heard
and told himself, "Why, it's absurd
to wish for what I can't receive!
To want peace when I see her grieve
because I struck her lord's death blow!
My word, you'd think I didn't know
she hates me more than any knight
on earth now, and with every right,
but I may well say 'now,' in part
1330 since women have one hundred hearts.
Despite her grief, it won't be strange
if, later on, she has a change
of heart. Indeed she will, I swear!
So I am foolish to despair.
God grant that she may change with speed.
I am her prisoner; Love's decreed,
and men who do not welcome Love
when she has come, are guilty of
misconduct and disloyalty.
1340 I say (no matter who hears me)
that such men ought to lose their right

[40]

to joy. I'll keep my own delight
and love my enemy always.
I know that hating her betrays
Love, and my duty has to be
to love the one Love chose for me.
Then, ought the lady to address
me as her friend? I love her; yes!
and yet 'my enemy' I name her:
She hates me, and I cannot blame her;   1350
I killed her lover. Can she contend
that I'm her foe? No! I'm her friend.
No lady ever was so fair.
I'm sorry for her lovely hair;
it shines more brightly than fine gold.
It makes me angry to behold
her hair torn out, and no one dries
the tears that flow down from her eyes;
these things torment and sadden me.
Although the tears flow endlessly,   1360
there never were such lovely eyes.
I feel so sad each time she cries!
I think that nothing will erase
my suffering when she claws her face.
It hasn't earned such injury!
I've seen no face so beautifully
aglow with color; every line
and feature's so well drawn and fine,
it breaks my heart to know that she
is now her face's enemy.   1370
Most certainly it's no pretense; she
is hurting herself so intensely,
but never did a crystal glass
or mirror shine more bright. Alas!
Why is it she cannot restrain
her grief and spare herself such pain?

[41]

Why does she wring her hands and strike
her breast? For wouldn't she be like
some natural wonder, beautiful

1380   to look upon, if she were full
of happiness, since she is so
exquisite in the depths of woe?
Oh, yes, indeed, I swear she would.
I think that Nature never could
surpass herself and duplicate
such loveliness. Who could create
this work of art? How was it done?
From where did such great beauty come?
Most surely God chose to create her

1390   with His bare hands, just to keep Nature
amused. If Nature tried to make
a replica, the task would take
all of her time and be in vain,
nor could God, if He tried again,
create a woman who would look
as fair, whatever pains He took!"

That's how the lord Yvain perceived
the lady as she wept and grieved.
But there will never be again

1400   a prisoner like the lord Yvain,
who thinks that he will lose his head,
but who is so in love, instead
of seeking pardon, makes no plea,
though no one will speak for him. He
sat by the window ledge, to stay
until the lady went away.
Now, when they dropped the sliding gate,
another might have mourned his fate,
if he desired most to obtain

1410   his freedom. But the lord Yvain

[42]

did not care if the gate door stayed
up or down. If the lady bade
him go; if, kindly, she acquitted
him of her lord's death; if they lifted
the palace gate, the lord Yvain
would not leave. Love and shame detain
the lord: he'd be ashamed to leave,
for then nobody would believe
his quest successful; also he
had such a great desire to see   1420
the lovely lady, if no more,
he did not mind his prison, for
he'd rather die than leave the palace.
But then the maid returned to solace,
to fetch and carry for him, be
amusing, and keep him company.
Because of the great love he bore,
he seemed more pensive than before
and tired. "What did you think of such
a day?" "I liked it very much."   1430
"My lord Yvain, what did you say?
How could you have a pleasant day
with killers searching in this room?
Why, you must love and seek your doom!"
"Most certainly," he said, "sweet friend,
I do not want my life to end.
Yet, as I stand before God, with awe,
I was most pleased with what I saw,
am pleased, and always will be pleased."
"Let's say no more of that!" she teased,   1440
as she well knew how to perceive
his meaning. "I'm not so naive
or foolish I can't understand
what you mean! Come with me now, and
I will arrange some strategy

[43]

that will set you at liberty
if not tonight, then by tomorrow.
I'll lead the way if you will follow."
"You may be certain," he replied,
1450   "I won't leave secretly, disguised
like some low thief. When all the men
have gathered in the town streets, then
I'll go, more honored, in full sight,
than if I'd sneaked away by night."
On saying this, the lord Yvain
went back to the small room again.
The maiden, who was very kind,
was quick to serve him and to find
and give him anything he chose.
1460   When, later on, the chance arose,
the maid recalled he'd said he'd been
well pleased by what he had seen, when
his enemies, who sought his doom,
were searching for him in the room.

The lady and the demoiselle
were close and got along so well,
the maiden did not fear to be
frank with her and speak openly,
regardless of how it might end.
1470   She was her confidante and friend,
so why should she fear to console
her lady or to take the role
of offering good advice? Instead,
the first time they could talk, she said,
"My lady, I'm amazed to see
you're acting so hysterically!
Do you believe that you can bring
your lord to life by sorrowing?"
"No," said the lady, "I wish, though,

[44]

that I myself could die of woe."   1480
"But why?" "To go the way he did."
"To go the way he . . . God forbid!
and send as good a lord to you,
which He does have the power to do."
"You've never told me such a lie
as 'God could send one as good'!" "Why,
He'll send one better, I've no doubt,
if you'll accept him." "Hush! Get out!
I won't find one as brave as he!"
"Oh, yes you will, if you'll agree!   1490
But tell me, who'll defend your land
next week? You know King Arthur's planned
to come and see the magic spring
and great stone. Start remembering
the way the Damsel in the Wild
warned you about him a short while
ago by letter. She was nice!
My lady, you must get advice.
You must defend your magic spring,
and you have not stopped sorrowing!   1500
Dear lady, please do not delay,
for all the knights you have today
aren't worth a single chambermaid:
the whole lot would be so afraid!
Your bravest knight could never wield
a lance or even touch a shield.
Oh, you have cowards, and to spare,
but no one brave enough to dare
to ride a horse, and so the king
will easily seize everything   1510
unchallenged, such a host has he!"
The lady knew well and could see
the maiden's counsel was sincere
and meant in good faith. But I fear

[45]

at times she acted foolishly
like other women: all can be
quite silly and at times refuse
the things they most want, when they choose.
The lady yielded to caprice.

1520 "Get out!" she said. "Leave me in peace!
If once again I hear you say
such awful things, you'll go away!"
"Until a better time," said she,
"You're a real woman, I can see,
for women flare up in a trice
when they are given good advice!"
The maid withdrew and let her be
alone in her great misery.
The lady soon became aware

1530 she'd been exceedingly unfair.
On second thought she wished to know
the way the maid had planned to show
that she could find a husband more
courageous than the one before,
and now she would have paid attention!
But she'd forbidden her to mention
the subject or to speak one word
of what she'd willingly have heard.
She waited with this thought in mind

1540 until the maid returned, to find
her prohibition was in vain.
At once the maid began again,
"You'd die of grief? Be more controlled,
my lady, you must be consoled.
For shame! Now you must overcome
your sorrow: it does not become
a gentlewoman of such worth
to disregard her noble birth
and reputation and to grieve

[46]

for so long! Now, do you believe 1550
all valor has died with your husband?
But men good as he ever was, and
some better men are still on earth!"
"If you aren't lying about his worth,
God strike me! Name one man who's shown
such valor as my lord was known
for all his life!" "You won't be grateful,
my lady, you'll become so hateful,
you'll start to threaten me again!"
"No, no, I promise. Please explain!" 1560
"I hope to Heaven it pleases you.
But if you will consent to do
what I suggest, then may it bring
you joy! Since no one's listening,
I don't believe I need to hold
my tongue, although I'm sure you'll scold.
But I may say, it seems to me,
when two knights meet, both equally
well armed for war, and test their might . . .
whom do you think the better knight, 1570
when one man beats the other one?
Now I think that the knight who won
should have the prize. What would you do?"
"I think that you are trying to
use my own words to capture me."
"My lady, surely you can see
that I can prove that I am right.
The man who is the better knight
than your lord is the man who's shown
that he could conquer him alone, 1580
and then was brave enough to chase
and shut him in his dwelling place!"
"Now you have had the most absurd
idea that I have ever heard!

Get out! You're full of wickedness!
And don't come back again unless
you'll never mention him to me!"
The maid said, "Lady, now you see.
I told you earlier I knew
1590 that I would have no thanks from you
for speaking so straightforwardly.
You said you'd not be cross with me,
and yet you haven't kept your word!
In spite of everything I heard,
you've said exactly what you will!
I've lost a good chance to keep still."

The maid went to the room again,
wherein she kept the lord Yvain
in utmost comfort at his leisure.
1600 But nothing gave him any pleasure.
The lady fair he could not see;
he knew no word of the maid's plea.
The lady too was very vexed.
She stayed awake all night, perplexed
about her fountain and ashamed
that she'd insulted and had blamed
the demoiselle so hatefully.
The lady knew her loyalty
and knew no love for him or base
1610 reward would make her plead his case
as she had done. The demoiselle
had loved her mistress far too well
to give her bad advice. It's strange,
her mind has undergone a change.
She whom she'd scolded so before,
she feared would hate her evermore,
and he whom she at first refused,
she now most loyally excused.

[48]

By reasoning, she proved the knight,
if brought to trial, would be right.   1620
The lady spoke as if he were
there, standing in the room with her.
Alone she started to debate:
"And so," she said, "will you negate
my husband and my lord is dead,
and that you caused his death?" she said.
He answered, "That I can't deny,
so I admit it." "Tell me why;
was it because of hatred, spite,
or to hurt me?" Replied the knight,   1630
"My lady, may death strike me too,
if I did it to injure you."
"You meant no harm to me then, nor
were you unjust to my lord, for
he'd have killed you. It seems to me
I have judged well and righteously."
She proved by her own arguments
she'd found truth, justice, and good sense.
She had no cause to hate the knight
and told herself that she was right   1640
to follow her desires. Unwooed,
she flamed with love in solitude
the way a smoking log, alone,
bursts into flame, though no one's blown
on it or stirred it. If the maid
had come in then, she would have swayed
the lady and have won the fight
in which she'd pleaded for the knight
so well and had received such blame.
Next morning, back the maiden came,   1650
took up her theme, said all she'd said
that night. The lady bowed her head,
because she knew she'd been unfair

[49]

to scold her. Now her only care
was asking pardon, and the station,
the lineage and reputation
and name of that brave knight, so she
was wise and answered quietly,
"I want to beg you to forgive
1660 the haughty and derogative
words that I spoke so foolishly.
I'll follow your advice. Tell me
what he is like, please, if you can,
and from what family is the man
for whom you pled so long. If he
is suitable and will agree,
I swear that I will wed him and
will make him master of my land,
but he must act in such a way
1670 that no one blames me, or can say,
'There is the lady; look at her!
She wed her husband's murderer!' "
"My lady, just as you think best!
You'll have the nicest, handsomest,
and noblest lord that ever came
from Abel's line!" "But what's his name?"
"The lord Yvain." "Why, he's the son
of King Urien! My word, he's one
of very noble birth, you know!"
1680 "My lady, yes; you know that's so."
"When can we see him?" "The fifth day
from now." "That's too long to delay;
I wish he were here now! The knight
must come tomorrow or tonight!"
"My lady, even birds can't fly
so far in just one day. But I
will send the squire they report

[50]

runs fastest to King Arthur's court,
where we must look for him. He might
arrive there by tomorrow night."   1690
"That's still too long to wait! The days
are long. What if the squire says,
'Please be there by tomorrow night'?
If he will force himself, the knight
could ride twice as far on the way,
and he could turn the night to day,
because that night the moon will shine.
When he arrives, he'll have of mine
whatever he would like," said she.
"My lady, leave it all to me.   1700
I'm sure you'll have the knight at hand
the day after tomorrow, and
tomorrow you must call your men
to seek advice, and tell them then
about the visit of the king.
In order to defend your spring
and keep the custom as it's been,
you need advice. None of your men
would dare to volunteer to fight,
and so you will have every right   1710
to say you must remarry, and
a splendid knight has sought your hand.
He's very suitable, but you've
not dared accept till they approve.
The cowards will approve your plan.
The chance to force another man
to bear a burden that they fear
to bear themselves can but appear
so welcome, that your men will fall
right down and thank you, one and all.   1720
Because of you they will be spared

[51]

great terror, for the man who's scared
by his own shadow shuns the chance
of meeting with a spear or lance.
A coward views such games with dread!"
"Oh yes, indeed," the lady said.
"I want it so and I consent.
In fact, I'd thought to some extent
of what you'd planned. That's what we'll do.
1730 But go now! Hurry! Why are you
delaying? Do as you've planned, then,
and I'll start summoning my men."

So here their conversation ended.
On the next day the maid pretended
that she'd dispatched the squire, and
that he would search throughout the land
for Sir Yvain. Each day the maid
saw that the lord Yvain was bathed
and helped him wash and comb his hair.
1740 She brought a red silk suit with vair
to line it, still chalkfilmed and new.
The maiden was most willing to
lend anything that would adorn
his clothes: a golden buckle worn
at the neck, set with stones so rare
that he seemed gracious, free from care;
a belt, and a fine alms purse made
of rich and costly gold brocade.
The lord Yvain was finely clad.
1750 Then she announced the squire had
returned from Arthur's court, and he
had acted well and prudently.
"But tell me when the lord Yvain
will come?" the lady asked again.

"He is here now," the maid replied.
"Already here? Send him inside
most secretly and privately,
when there is no one here with me.
Be sure there's no one else allowed;
I do think four would be a crowd." 1760
The maid left her alone again
and went to fetch the lord Yvain.
She made sure that her face concealed
her heartfelt joy, and she revealed
instead her lady'd learned that day
that she had hidden him away.
She said, "Good Heavens, Sir Yvain,
to hide this now would be in vain,
for things have gone so far, I fear
my lady knows that you are here, 1770
and how she blamed and hated me,
and scolded and berated me!
But finally she gave her word
that I could bring you in, assured
of safe-conduct. Don't be alarmed,
I do not think you will be harmed,
but I don't wish to be deceiving,
to lie or keep you from believing
she wants you in her prison cell,
your body and your heart as well." 1780
The lord Yvain said, "Certainly,
that won't be difficult for me;
I want to be her prisoner."
"By my right hand, you may be sure
you will be! Come now, let us seek
the lady. But you must be meek
before her, lest your prison be made
too harsh! But do not be afraid;

[53]

I do not think that you will find
1790   your prison an unpleasant kind."

At this, the maiden took him in,
dismaying and reassuring him
and telling him mysteriously
about the prison where he'd be.
However she is right to call
the lord a prisoner: lovers all
are prisoners: no one can be
truly in love and yet be free.
So, by the hand, she led the lord
1800   Yvain in where he was adored,
although he feared he would be greeted
with hate. They found the lady seated
on a huge cushion of bright red.
The lord Yvain was filled with dread;
so frightened he dared not draw near.
Her silence magnified his fear.
He thought that he had been betrayed.
He froze and for so long delayed,
the maiden lost her self-control.
1810   "Five hundred curses on the soul
of anyone who dares presume
to bring to a fair lady's room
a tongueless knight who gives offense
by lacking manners and the sense
to introduce himself!" The maid
reached for his arm. "Don't be afraid!
Not of my lady; she won't bite,
just go and ask for peace, Sir knight!
I hope she will forgive you for
1820   her husband's death, her dear, dead lord,
Sir Esclados the Red." Yvain
clasped his hands together, came,

[54]

and knelt before her, but, instead,
he truly loved her, so he said,
"My lady, I will not implore
your mercy; I will thank you, for
I know I could not feel dismay
or be displeased in any way
by anything you wish to do."
"Oh, no, sir? What if I kill you?"   1830
"I'll thank you," said the lord Yvain.
"You never will hear me complain."
"I've never heard of this," she said.
"You are prepared to risk your head
and to be in my power, though
no one has forced you to do so!"
"My lady, no one's force could be
as strong as the force which orders me
to yield completely to your will;
I'm not afraid, I would fulfill   1840
whatever order you might say.
Besides, if I could find a way
to make amends for all the pain
I caused you when your lord was slain,
I'd gladly do so." "What? Tell me,
before I grant indemnity
from my lord's death, if all along
to hurt me and to do me wrong
was really what you had in mind?"
"My lady," he replied, "be kind.   1850
Your lord had started to attack;
why was I wrong to fight him back?
For if a warrior intends
to catch and kill one who defends
himself and kills in self defense,
would you deny his innocence?"
"No, if you view it as you should.

To have you killed would do no good.
But I would like to know the source
1860   and origin of that rare force
which has ordained that you consent
to my will with no argument.
I pardon your misdeeds; you're free.
Now, come sit down here next to me
and tell me why you are so tame?"
He said, "My lady, the force came
out of my heart, for it is set
upon you and is in your debt;
my heart has given me this desire."
1870   "Please tell me what things could inspire
your heart to do so, my sweet friend?"
"Lady, my eyes." "What your eyes, then?"
"The perfect beauty they behold
in you." "Then do you plan to scold
the beauty for it?" "Yes, I do;
it's made me love. . . ." "Whom?" "I love you,
dear lady." "Me?" "Yes." "In what way?"
"I love you more than I can say;
in such a way a love more deep
1880   cannot exist. My heart will keep
close to yours and will never stray,
for I love you in such a way
that I can think of nothing else;
I love you far more than myself;
I'm wholly yours; I've pledged today
to yield to you and to obey
all your commands. I'm willing to
live if you wish or die for you."
"And would you dare to undertake
1890   defending my fountain for my sake?"
"My lady, yes; against all men."

[56]

"Know we are well agreed."

So then
they reached a swift accord. Besides,
the lady had been well advised
by her knights and her barons, so
she said to him, "From here we'll go
into the hall, where my liege men
are waiting for us. They have been
advising me to marry, since
we need protection badly. Hence   1900
I shall do so; I do not choose
to look more: I should not refuse
to take as my lord anyone
who is a brave knight and a king's son."
And now the lady has acquired
exactly what her heart desired.
The lord Yvain was not offended,
I may tell you, that she intended
to take him with her to the hall,
now filled with knights and squires. All   1910
the men found Sir Yvain so fair
and noble that they paused to stare
in admiration, then the crowd
of men rose to their feet and bowed.
Each man politely bent his head
to greet the lord Yvain, and said,
"Our lady'll wed this man, and ill
to him who goes against her will;
he seems a splendid man to me.
The Roman empress would be   1920
well wed to him. Would that she were
betrothed to him, and he to her,
with bare hands joined, and would that they
were wed tomorrow or today."

[57]

The lady went on down the hall,
to let them see her, one and all,
and found a bench on which she sat.
The lord Yvain pretended that
he would sit at her feet. But she
1930   told him to rise immediately
and beckoned for her seneschal,
so he'd be heard throughout the hall.
At once the seneschal began,
he was no shy or stubborn man.
"My lords, we are at war. Each day
the king prepares his knights to lay
waste to our land. If no brave knight
will come within two weeks to fight,
all this will be destroyed. You know
1940   that almost seven years ago,
our lady, by your leave, was wed.
She is so sad her lord is dead.
He who was master of this land
and its adornment can command
no more now than a garden plot.
It's such a pity he did not
live longer! But no woman wants
to bear a shield and use a lance,
so she would be much better for
1950   a marriage with some worthy lord,
nor could there be a greater need.
Advise her to be wed with speed,
and in this way she'll have maintained
the castle's custom. It's remained
unbroken over sixty years."

When he was through, the knights and peers
exclaimed his plan seemed excellent,

[58]

increased her will by their consent,
and threw themselves down at her feet.
The lady made her men entreat   1960
her to do what she wished, until,
as if it were against her will,
she said she'd do what she'd have done,
were she opposed by everyone.
She said, "My lords, since you decree,
this knight who's sitting next to me
has begged to marry me, intending
to do me honor by defending
my castle. I thank him, and you
must be most grateful to him, too.   1970
I've never known him personally,
but I've heard much about him. He
is very noble, gentlemen;
his father is King Urien.
And more than being of high birth,
he has, in battle, proved his worth,
and shown such courtesy and respect,
no one could possibly object.
I think you all have heard his name:
my suitor is the lord Yvain,   1980
a lord of nobler family
than I am, when he marries me!"

The lady's men said, "If you're wise,
we think that you will realize
the marriage should take place today,
for it is foolish to delay
a worthy action." They implored
till she agreed to wed the lord.
That's what she'd have done anyway!
For Love commands the marriage they   1990

[59]

had been requested to consider.
But their approval only did her
honor, and their prayers inspired
her to do as her heart desired
and grant its wishes and its need,
the way a quickly moving steed
would gallop even faster, were
it prodded by its rider's spur.

The lady promised them and said
2000   the lord Yvain and she would wed
that day. So, from her chaplain's hand
the lord Yvain received her, and
he wed the lady of Landuc,
who was the daughter of the duke
Laududez, of whom they sing the lay,
without delay, that very day.
The lord saw many a crook and miter;
the lady'd chosen to invite her
bishops and her abbots to
2010   her wedding. Many guests came, who
were nobly born and happier
than I could tell you if I were
to think more of it! I'll refrain
from saying more. The lord Yvain
is master now. The dead man's been
forgotten since the moment when
the very knight who took his life
had courted and had wed his wife.
They sleep together. All adore
2020   and prize the living man far more
than their dead lord. With much good will
the wedding feast went on until
the night before the day the king
came to the wondrous stone and spring.

[60]

KING ARTHUR undertook that ride
with friends and household at his side,
for almost no one chose to stay
behind. And then up spoke Sir Kay,
"My God, whatever has become
of Sir Yvain, who didn't come,   2030
and after dinner bragged that he'd
avenge his cousin? Yes, indeed,
he spoke when he'd drunk wine. I swear
he's run away; he didn't dare
to come with us and chose to hide
when he had boasted with such pride!
How brave is he who dares to flaunt
deeds other men would scarcely want
to mention, with no evidence
but flattery! What a difference   2040
between the coward and brave man!
The coward by the fireplace can
say much about himself, for he
thinks other men are fools who'd be
too dull to know how much he's lied.
The brave man would be mortified
if he should hear somebody mention
his deeds to others. My contention
is that the coward's right to vaunt
his valiant deeds; who else would want   2050
to talk about them? Heralds fall
still round the coward, and they all
proclaim the brave deeds of the bold
and leave the coward in the cold.
The coward finds nobody to
tell lies for him. A fool he who

[61]

admires himself for hidden good,
but won't boast of it, as he should!"
Those were the words of the lord Kay.
2060   The lord Gawain was quick to say,
"Enough, my lord Kay! Anyhow,
the lord Yvain is not here now,
and you don't know the reason why.
Some urgent task may occupy
his time. I know the lord Yvain
would not debase himself or deign
to call you such vile names, for he
is noted for his courtesy."
"Sir," Kay replied, "I'll say no more
2070   about it and be quiet, for
I see it bothers you." King Arthur
had spilled a basin full of water
upon the stone to see the rain.
The storm broke. Soon the lord Yvain
was fully armed. He turned to seize
his sword and galloped through the trees
and rode ahead at breakneck speed
upon a great, courageous steed,
bold, swift, and powerful. That day
2080   it happened that it was Sir Kay
who asked the honor of the fight.
Things could end any way they might,
but Sir Kay wanted to commence
the fighting at all tournaments,
or else he would start grumbling.
He came on foot before the king
and asked to be allowed to fight.
"Sir Kay," King Arthur told the knight,
"since you want to and asked before
2090   the others, there's no reason for
denying you this favor." Kay

KNIGHT WITH THE LION

thanked him, mounted, and rode away.
But in this fight, if Sir Yvain
could cause embarrassment and pain
to Kay, he'd gladly do him harm.
He'd recognized Kay by his arms.
And so the lord Yvain and Kay
took their shields by the straps, and they
drew back, then rushed together, spurred
their horses onward, and secured   2100
their lances, which both knights held tightly.
They thrust their lances forward slightly
so that they held them by the leather
butts, and when they came together,
the knights struck such hard blows, each shaft
was split in two back to the haft.
The lord Yvain struck such a blow,
Kay fell back over the saddle bow
and tumbled head first to the ground.
At once the lord Yvain got down   2110
from his horse, since he knew that he
would do no further injury
to Kay. He took Kay's horse instead,
which pleased the knights. They laughed and said,
"Well, look at this! Here lies the knight
who was so scornful! Still, it's right
to pardon you this one time, for
it's not been done to you before!"
The lord Yvain went to the king.
He led Kay's horse up, managing   2120
him by the reins and saying, "Sire,
please take the horse; I've no desire
to keep him, for I would be wrong
to take something that must belong
to you." "Who are you?" In reply
the king said, "I can't tell you by

your voice, if I can't see your face,
or you don't say your name." His grace
the lord Yvain told them his name,
2130 and Sir Kay nearly died of shame,
for he had been the one to say
the lord Yvain had run away.
The courtiers were exceedingly
delighted by his victory.
The king was pleased. But they attest,
one hundred times more than the rest,
the victory pleased the lord Gawain,
who loved his comrade, Sir Yvain,
more than all other knights he'd known.
2140 The king requested to be shown
how Sir Yvain had come to be
the warrior at the spring and tree.
The king was curious to know
the truth about what happened, so
the lord Yvain began to tell
the kindness of the demoiselle
and didn't leave out anything.
When he was done, he asked the king
and all his knights and men to ride
2150 on to the town. The king replied
that he would visit Sir Yvain
with greatest pleasure. He'd remain
in town and give him one week of
joy and his company and love.
When Sir Yvain had thanked the king,
they did not linger by the spring;
they mounted their great steeds and rode
along the fastest, smoothest road
into the town. The lord Yvain
2160 dispatched a squire with a crane-

falcon, so the lady would
not be surprised, and her men could
bedeck their houses for the king.
When she heard Sir Yvain would bring
the king and court to visit, she
was joyful and exceedingly
pleased by the news. The lady said
that all her men should ride ahead
and meet the king. Her men were so
delighted, no one answered no;   2170
they did her will with utmost speed.
Each mounted his great Spanish steed,
and met the king of Britain, and
politely welcomed to the land
King Arthur and his knights that day.
"Sire, welcome, welcome to this way
which is so full of valiant men,
and blessed be he who's leading them,
and bringing us such splendid guests!"

When the king came, the bells expressed   2180
the people's joy and jubilation.
They had hung out for decoration
their finest silken draperies.
The streets were spread with tapestries
upon the pavement for the king.
The people had had time to string
up awnings in the town streets, made
to guarantee the king had shade.
The sound of trumpet, bell, and horn
made the town ring so, I'd have sworn   2190
you'd not have heard God thunder. Drums
and cymbals, flutes and kettledrums,
and different kinds of pipes were played

before the staircase where the maids
descended. On the other side
were lightly leaping youths. They tried
to show their joy, and suitably
they greeted their king joyously.
Next came the lady of the town,
2200   dressed in a regal ermine gown.
The lady wore upon her head
a ruby diadem, bright red.
The lady's face seemed in no way
annoyed; she smiled and was so gay,
I think no countess has appeared
as beautiful. The people cheered,
"Long live the king, king of kings and
of all the lords throughout the land!"
At first the king could not reply.
2210   He saw the lady coming by
to hold his stirrup. Instantly
the king got down himself, and she
began to greet him, "Welcome, Sire,
a thousand times, and I desire
to welcome here to our domain
King Arthur's nephew, Sir Gawain."
The king said, "Lovely thing, I pray
your face and body always may
have joy and luck!" The king embraced
2220   the lovely lady round the waist
most courteously and heartily.
She hugged him with both arms. There'll be
no more description of the way
she welcomed all her guests that day.
No one has honored any guest
with such delight and joy and zest.
I'd tell you more about their bliss,
but I can't waste my words like this!

[66]

But I would like to say one word
about a meeting which occurred   2230
in private, with the moon and sun.
Do you know whom I mean? The one
who was the lord of knights, acclaimed
above all knights, may well be named
the sun—the lord Gawain—for he
illuminated chivalry,
the way that morning sunlight bathes
with light each place it casts its rays.
And she whom I have called the moon—
there is but one so opportune   2240
because of her great constancy.
Not only do I say that she
is called the moon for worth and fame,
but also, "Lunette" was her name.

The charming maid was named Lunette:
she was a courteous brunette,
discreet and clever. She became
acquainted with the lord Gawain,
who liked her and admired her. He
called her his sweetheart, knowing she   2250
had saved his friend from death. They say
the lord Gawain pledged, from that day,
to serve Lunette. She'd been describing
the trouble she had overriding
her lady's worries, so she'd wed
the lord Yvain, and then she said
that when the men had wished to kill
the lord, he'd been invisible!
The lord Gawain went into gales
of laughter when he heard her tales.   2260
"Mademoiselle, I give to you,
when you don't need me, when you do,

[67]

a champion such as I am.
Don't trade me for a better man,
if you think you'll improve your score!
For I am yours, and evermore
you must be my maid." "Sir," said she,
"I thank you for your courtesy!"
So went the meeting of these two!

2270 The other courtiers flirted too,
for there were ninety ladies: each
was beautiful and fair of speech,
well bred, and courteous, and fine,
a lady of a noble line
and gentle birth, so it was right
that all the men could take delight
in the fair ladies' conversation,
could look at them with admiration,
could sit with them, kiss them, and touch
2280 their hands. At least they had that much!
How happy was the lord Yvain!
The king had chosen to remain
in his house, and his wife received
each guest so well, some fools believed
the gracious lady was inspired
by Love, who always has required
such conduct. Such a man's naive,
when ladies greet him, to believe
they love him, when they're so polite,
2290 and speak to some unlucky knight,
and gladden him with hug and kiss.
To fools a pretty speech is bliss;
Too soon they credit all who speak.
They spent a most delightful week.
The woods and rivers offered sport
to any members of the court

who wished to hunt and fish there, and
whoever wished to see the land
that had been won by Sir Yvain
with his fair lady, could remain   2300
for some time traveling around
to towns and mansions that he found
within the radius of four
or five or six full leagues or more.

GAWAIN RECALLS YVAIN TO CHIVALRY

AT the week's end, the king had stayed
as long as he desired and made
his plans to leave the town. The throng
of courtiers, the whole week long,
had begged and urged the lord Yvain
to go with them. The lord Gawain   2310
said, "What! Will you be like those, then,
who have become less valiant men,
and once that they have taken wives,
are worth less for it all their lives?
Shame on those warriors, by Saint Mary,
who grow less valiant when they marry!
A man should lead a better life,
when he has taken as a wife,
or mistress too, a lady fair.
You know that he would never dare   2320
to say he has the right to claim
her love when he has lost his fame
and reputation. Surely you
would start to grow resentful too,
if you became a lesser man
for loving her! A woman can
not be thought wrong if she withdrew

her admiration once she knew
and scorned the suitor who became
2330   less as the lord of her domain.
Your reputation must not falter!
Slip off the bridle and the halter
and come to tournaments with me,
lest you be charged with jealousy!
No, no, you must not hesitate,
but come to tourneys, participate,
use all your force and all your might,
whatever it costs you to fight.
He dreams all day who does not act!
2340   Indeed you must come, and in fact
I'll hear no more excuses! Fair
comrade-in-arms, you must take care:
be sure our friendship does not end
because of you. You know, my friend,
it will not end because of me.
I wonder why a man can be
so anxious to obtain and seize
a never-ending life of ease,
for joys grow greater when delayed:
2350   small pleasures frequently are made
to taste much sweeter, with delay,
than ecstasy enjoyed today.
The joy of loves that come but later
seems like the green log which gives greater
heat when it's burned and lasts all night,
though it takes longer to ignite.
It isn't difficult to make
bad habits that are hard to shake,
and when you try to break away,
2360   you can't! Although I wouldn't say
all this as firmly as I do,
had I as fair a love as you,

[70]

dear friend Yvain. Indeed yes, by
my faith in God and His saints, I
would leave her most unhappily.
In fact I know that I would be
a fool about her. I give good
advice to others that I would
not take myself, just like a priest:
disloyal lechers, but at least   2370
they tell us what is right, and teach,
but do not practice what they preach!"

For a long time the lord Gawain
implored until the lord Yvain
agreed to ask his wife to say
he had her leave to go away.
From wisdom or from foolishness,
he'd ask his lady to say yes
and let him go to Britain. He
went to discuss it with her. She   2380
had no idea he wished to go.
"My dearest lady, as you know,
you are my happiness, my wealth,
my heart, my very soul, my health.
Grant me one thing you'll find to be
an honor both for you and me."
At once the lady gave consent,
with no idea of what he meant
to ask, and said, "My lord, decree
whatever you desire of me."   2390
He asked leave to accompany
King Arthur and his court. Then he
would go on to the tournament,
so none could call him indolent.
The lady said, "I give you leave
to go there, but you must believe,

if you outstay a certain date,
my love for you will turn to hate,
you may be sure, if you're away
2400   for longer than the time I say.
I do not lie: if you decline
to keep your word, I will keep mine.
So if you wish to keep my love;
if you love me at all; above
all else, remember to be here
again, at least within a year.
Today's one week past Saint John's feast.
If you are not back by at least
that day a year hence, or before,
2410   I will not love you anymore."
The lord Yvain began to cry
so hard he scarcely could reply,
"To be away from you one year!
Were I a dove, I would be here
with you so often! And I pray
that God will not keep me away
so long, but though a man may mean
to come home soon, some unforeseen
thing keeps him. I can't contemplate
2420   the future, and I might be late
because I had an urgent reason,
like prison, illnesses, or treason.
You're not fair to refuse to see
I might be hindered physically."
"My lord, I'm making that exception.
And yet, if God grants you protection
from death, you need have no concern;
nothing will hinder your return
as long as you remember me,
2430   that I can promise faithfully.
I will lend you my ring to wear

[72]

upon your finger, and I'll share
the nature of the stone with you.
A loyal lover who is true
will not become misfortune's prey,
will not be hurt, and will not stay
in any prison, if above
all else, he thinks about his love
and wears the ring upon his hand.
You will be like an iron band.   2440
The ring will be your mail and shield.
Now I have never wished to yield
the ring to any knight I knew,
but I am lending it to you
because I love you." He had leave
to go, but he began to grieve
and weep at leaving her. The king
would not postpone his traveling,
no matter what they said, of course.
He wanted to have every horse   2450
equipped and bridled, every one.
As soon as he spoke, it was done.
They brought the palfreys ready to ride.
I haven't managed to decide
whether I should or shouldn't say
how Sir Yvain then rode away
with many kisses mixed with tears
and steeped in sweetness. It appears
I'd take too long if I went farther
and told the escort of King Arthur: 2460
the lady came and brought with her
all of the maids and knights there were.
The lady wept. King Arthur then
told her to turn back with her men
to her town, and he urged her so,
she turned back with the greatest woe.

[73]

The lord Yvain was so bereft
when his love turned back, that he left
his heart with her. The king could take
2470   his body, but he could not make
his heart come too, for by Love's art
the lady clung tight to his heart,
and all King Arthur's power and sway
could never take his heart away.
We know the body can't survive
without a heart, yet he's alive!
His body has no heart inside!
So it can never be denied
that such a wonder came about,
2480   because he's still alive without
his heart, which, though enclosed before,
will not go with him anymore.
The heart has a good home. They say
the body must live for the day
it joins its heart. It tries to cope
by fashioning a heart of hope:
a strange heart, frequently a cheat,
and full of treason and deceit.
Now I believe the lord Yvain
2490   will find he cannot ascertain
the moment when he is betrayed
by hope, for if he overstayed
one day the year that they agreed,
the lord would find it hard indeed
to earn forgiveness, and I fear
that he will overstay the year.
The lord Gawain will not consent
to let him leave. The two knights went
to tournaments, where and whenever
2500   the tournaments were held, together,
and in this manner every day

[74]

of that year quickly passed away.
The whole year long, the lord Yvain
fought so well, that the lord Gawain
both honored him and made him stay
so long, the whole year slipped away,
and part of next year too, they claim,
until the king, when August came,
held court at Chester, where they went
the night before from a tournament.   2510
The lord Yvain, so I surmise
from what I've heard, won every prize.
Because the two knights did not care
to lodge in town, the two had their
tents pitched outside the city gate
and held their own court there, in state.
They did not go to the king's court;
the king came to theirs. By report,
they had with them the very best
of Arthur's knights, and as their guest   2520
the king sat in the midst of all.

YVAIN'S MADNESS

THEN Sir Yvain chanced to recall,
and never, since the very day
he'd left his wife and gone away,
was he so utterly undone
by any thought as by this one—
he had not kept the vow he'd made.
He realized he'd overstayed
by weeks the limit of his year.
He found that he was close to tears,   2530
but, much ashamed, he thought and held

[75]

himself in check till he beheld
a maiden riding on a fleet
black palfrey which had pure white feet.
The maid dismounted at their tent,
and no one helped her down or went
to take her horse. Before them all
the maiden let her mantle fall,
when she had seen the king, and went
2540   displayed in this way in the tent,
and came to the king. The maid repeated
her message: that the lady greeted
King Arthur and the lord Gawain
and everyone except Yvain:
Yvain the liar, the untrue,
deceitful, cunning traitor, who
had tricked and wronged her, and now she
had realized his treachery!
Yvain had seemed true, and had said
2550   he loved her truly, but instead,
Yvain, just like a lying thief,
seduced her, and with disbelief,
the lady'd realized this, though she
had not suspected treachery,
and would have been the last to say
that he would steal her heart away.
True lovers don't steal hearts. But there
are men called low thieves everywhere,
who like to make love, but who know
2560   nothing about real love. Although
the lover takes his lady's heart,
he never steals the slightest part,
but treasures it and guards it. Then
the thieves, who seem like honest men,
but who are hypocrites, and cheat,
and steal, and lie, like to compete

[76]

by stealing hearts for which they care
nothing. The lover, everywhere
he goes, holds dear the heart he's won
and brings it back when his trip's done.   2570
Yvain has killed the lady. She
thought that with him, her heart would be
kept safely and returned some day
before the year had passed away.
Yvain, forgetful man, we find
you could not manage to remind
yourself you promised to appear
before my lady in a year!
She gave you leave to be away
until Saint John the Baptist's Day.   2580
You've no respect for her; you were
unable to remember her!
Within her room, for every day
and season, as it passed away,
my lady made a mark; for those
who love are ill at ease; they doze,
wake, count, and add up every day
that comes and finally goes away.
So loyal lovers count the days
and seasons, and she did not raise   2590
complaint before the proper day,
nor do I ask for trial. I say
the maid betrayed us when she wed
my lady to you, and she said
she cares for you no longer. Learn
she bids you never to return
and not to keep her ring. By me
whom you see here before you, she
commands you to give up the ring
and send it back to her, a thing   2600
that you are bound to do. Yvain

[77]

did not reply, for he became
devoid of reason and of speech.
The maiden sprang at him to reach
his hand and snatch away the ring.
She left in God's good care the king
and everyone except Yvain,
and him she left in dreadful pain,
and everything he saw and heard
2610   increased the torture he endured.
He wished to flee to some wild land
alone, where no one knew him and
could know where they could seek him out;
where nobody who knew about
him, man or woman, could obtain
a word of news about Yvain,
no more than if he'd been ill-fated
and fallen in a chasm. He hated
himself above all else. Although
2620   he was near death, he did not know
one soul to comfort him. Yvain
began to want to be insane,
because he could not find a way
to hurt himself and so to pay
for having lost his happiness.
Yvain arose in great distress
and left the barons far behind,
because he feared he'd lose his mind
among them. All the knights that day
2630   allowed Yvain to go away
and did not try to stop him, for
they realized he cared no more
for their talk and their company.
They let him go alone, and he
walked on and on until he went
far past each canopy and tent.

A whirlwind broke loose in his brain,
so violent that he went insane,
and clawed himself, tore off his clothes,
and fled across the fields and rows.   2640
He left his servants lost behind.
Astonished, they tried hard to find
Yvain and sought him left and right,
in orchards, houses where at night
the warriors in the town would stay,
and hedgerows, but he ran away,
until he came to a small field,
and met a boy, and made him yield
the bows and arrows in his hand.
Yvain stole five sharp arrows and   2650
the boy's bow. He remembered none
of all these things that he had done.
Once in the wood, he lay in wait
for animals, killed them, and ate
their flesh uncooked, completely raw,
like a wild man, until he saw
a hermit's hut, quite small and low.
The hermit was clearing land, and so
he saw the naked man about.
The hermit knew without a doubt   2660
the man was mad, and he was right;
Yvain had lost his mind. In fright
the hermit ran away and shut
himself inside his little hut.
But then the good man went ahead
and put fresh water and some bread
outside the hut upon the edge
of a small window's narrow ledge
for charity. The lord Yvain
was ravenous, and so he came,   2670
and seized the bread, and ate as much

[79]

as he could. He'd not tasted such
hard, bitter bread before, I'm sure.
The hermit's bread had grain so poor,
that it was sourer than yeast,
straw mixed with barley, and at least
one bushel only cost a shilling!
But pangs of hunger made him willing
to eat the bark-dry, musty bread
2680 the hermit gave him, and instead
it seemed to him like a nutritious
sauce, for hunger's a delicious
and well-made sauce for any food.
He ate the bread, and as he chewed,
he drank fresh water from the urn.
Once fed, Yvain left to return
into the wood and hunt for deer.
The hermit offered a sincere
prayer when he saw the madman go.
2690 He prayed the Lord God would bestow
protection on the lord Yvain
and not let him come back again.
But anyone, however few
his wits may be, will come back to
a place where he remembers he
was treated well, most willingly.
So, while the lord Yvain was mad,
not one whole week passed that he had
not caught some sort of wild beast for
2700 the hermit or come to his door.

Yvain so lived. The good man took
and skinned the animals to cook
part of the venison. The bread
and urn of water were kept spread
outside upon the window sill,

106-121

Sharpin' of the
Mountain

Bravery vs.
Cowardly

Lord Kay

so the madman could eat his fill.
That's what he had to drink and eat:
cold water from the spring and meat,
no salt, no pepper. To provide
for him, the hermit sold the hide   2710
and bought Yvain unleavened bread
of oats and barley. He was fed
on large amounts of bread and meat
the hermit gave to him to eat,
for many days, until at last
a lady with two maidens passed
through the wood, and the women found
Yvain asleep upon the ground.

THE LADY OF NORÍSON

ONE of the maids dismounted, ran
to where she'd seen the naked man,   2720
and looked him over carefully.
She saw nothing about him she
could use to recognize him, though
she'd seen him many times. I know
she would have known him instantly
if he'd worn his fine clothes, as he
had done so many times. The maid
did not know who he was. She stayed
and looked at him for a long space,
until at last upon his face   2730
she saw a scar. How well she knew
the lord Yvain had a scar too,
upon his face. The demoiselle
had seen Yvain's scar and knew well
he was Yvain. Though she was sure,

[81]

she wondered why she found him poor
and naked. Much astonished, she
made signs of the cross repeatedly,
but did not touch or wake Yvain.

2740   The maiden mounted her horse again,
and joined the others, and between
her sobs, she told them what she'd seen.
I don't know if I should delay
by telling you of their dismay.
In tears the maid tried to explain,
"My lady, I have found Yvain,
who's proved that he is of such worth
that he's the greatest knight on earth.
I can't imagine what sin might

2750   have brought the man to such a plight!
He must have suffered some great woe
which made him hold himself so low,
for people lose their minds from grief.
You will agree with my belief
that he is mad! He'd never be
behaving so indecently
if first he had not lost his mind.
I wish that God would help him find
his wits again, the best that he

2760   has ever had, so he'd agree
to come to your assistance, for
Count Alier, who is at war
with you, has struck too frequently.
Now, I would like this war to be
won by your side, if the good Lord
would help you, and if He restored
Yvain's mind, so that he agreed
to help you in this time of need."
The lady said, "If he'll just stay,

2770   with God's help we can find a way

[82]

to take this storm and madness out
of his head. We must go about
it now! I have a magic balm.
Morgan the Wise said it would calm
and cure the worst insanity
the day she sent this salve to me."

At once the ladies headed for
their castle, which was near: no more
than half of one full league away,
but counting by the leagues which they   2780
have in that land, for in this instance,
two of their leagues as we mark distance
are one league, and four two. Yvain
kept sleeping in the place he'd lain,
alone. Meanwhile the lady went
to her home for the liniment.
The lady opened up a case,
took a box from its hiding place,
and gave it to the maid. She said
to salve his temples and his head,   2790
but not to be too lavish: just
the head and temples, and she must
conserve the extra balm with care.
"There's no use putting it elsewhere;
except his head, there's nothing wrong
with him." The lady sent along
a red silk coat and cloak, a vair
fur robe: she'd have the maiden bear
these garments back. In her right hand
she led a splendid palfrey, and   2800
from her own store of clothes she chose
to add a fine shirt, and black hose,
and well-made pants, and then the maid
returned and found Yvain had stayed

[83]

asleep where she'd left him. She tied
her palfrey tightly to one side
in an enclosure, and she went
up to him with the liniment
and clothes. She overcame her fear
2810   of the madman, and she drew near,
till she could touch him with her hand.
The maid took up the ointment and
anointed him till none remained,
because she so hoped she'd obtained
a cure for him. She did not spare
the balm, but put it everywhere
with a free hand. She did not heed
the lady's warning, for indeed
the extra ointment was used well,
2820   or so she thought. The demoiselle
rubbed ointment on his head, then chose
to salve his body to the toes.
She rubbed and rubbed him with her palm
until the hot sun and the balm
drove out the madness in his brain.
How foolish to anoint Yvain
down to the toes! There's no need for
excessive cures! With five pints more
balm I know she'd have done the same.
2830   She took the box and fled; she came
and hid by her horse, but contrived
to leave the clothes; if he revived,
she wanted him to see the cloak
and put it on. By a great oak
the maiden waited till Yvain
had slept enough time to regain
his senses and his memory.
As naked as an ivory
when he revived, completely cured,

[84]

he was embarrassed; rest assured,   2840
if he'd known what occurred before,
he would have been so even more.
The lord Yvain did not know why
he was nude; seeing the supply
of clothes, he wondered how they came
to be there. He was filled with shame
about his nakedness. He said
indeed he was betrayed and dead
if anyone he knew had seen
him there. Then he put on the clean   2850
new clothes and looked off toward the wood
for travelers. As best he could,
he struggled to arise and stand,
but found he could not walk well, and
could hardly stand upon his feet.
He needed help and hoped to meet
some traveler. He had to seek
help; his misfortunes left him weak.
The maiden chose not to delay,
and so she rode along the way   2860
pretending that he wasn't there.
She passed close by. He did not care
who helped him, for his need was so
great that he only wished to go
and lodge somewhere he could regain
his strength. He called with might and main.
The maiden looked first left, then right,
as if she wondered where he might
be found. She rode as if confused,
this way and that, and she refused   2870
to go straight towards him, not at all.
The lord Yvain began to call,
"Come over here, mademoiselle,
come over this way!" At his yell,

[85]

the maiden tugged her palfrey's rein,
and she walked slowly toward Yvain.
She made him think she'd never known
or seen him, and the maid was shown
to have good manners and aplomb
2880   by this pretense. When she had come
close to the lord, she said, "What plight
has made you call for me, Sir knight?"
Said Sir Yvain, "I cannot tell
by what bad luck, mademoiselle,
I find I'm in this wood today.
By God and by your faith, I pray
you'll give or lend me, in my need,
at any price, that splendid steed
that you are leading." "Certainly,
2890   Sir knight," she said, "but come with me
where I am going." "Where are you
bound for?" "Out of this forest to
a town that you will find nearby."
"Mademoiselle, please tell me why.
Is it that you have need of me?"
"Indeed I do, Sir knight," said she.
"But I think you aren't in the best
of health, and so you ought to rest
for two weeks with us in our land.
2900   Now take this horse from my right hand,
and let's go to the castle door."

He could have asked for nothing more.
He took the horse. The lord Yvain
and maiden rode until they came
to a bridge at a turbulent,
swift-flowing stream. The maiden went
to throw the empty box away

into the stream, for in this way
she thought that she might be excused
for all the ointment she had used.   2910
She planned to say her palfrey tripped
upon the bridge, and the box slipped
from her hands, by ill luck, and fell
into the stream, and she as well
all but fell in, which would have been
a greater loss. The maiden then
invented this great lie to calm
her lady's wrath about the balm.
They rode on, as they had before,
until they reached the castle door.   2920
The lady met the lord Yvain,
whom she was pleased to entertain,
but when they were alone, she went
to ask her for the liniment
and box. The maiden in reply
repeated to her the great lie
she'd made up, for she was afraid
to tell her the whole truth. Dismayed,
the lady answered, very cross,
"This really is a dreadful loss,   2930
and what is even worse, it's plain
the box will not be found again!
But there is nothing to be done,
since it has happened. Often one
thinks to work for his benefit
and finds himself the worse for it.
I looked at him and saw ahead
my joy and wealth. I've lost, instead,
the rarest thing that I possess.
I want to tell you, nonetheless,   2940
to serve the man in every way."

[87]

"Oh, lady, that's what you should say,
for it would be a bad trick to
turn one misfortune into two."

They did not mention it again.
They took care of the lord Yvain
in every way they could. They bathed him,
and washed his head of hair, and shaved him,
and clipped his hair. You could have sheared

2950 a fistful of hair from his beard.
His every wish was gratified.
The ladies hastened to provide
arms, and a great, bold, handsome steed,
when he informed them he would need
a horse and armor. Sir Yvain
stayed at the castle to remain
at rest until Count Alier
attacked one Tuesday, so they say,
with all his knights and all his squires.

2960 They looted and they started fires.
The men in town heard the alarms,
arose, and equipped themselves with arms.
Unarmed and armed, they went to meet
the looters, who did not retreat.
The looters gathered in a mass
and waited for them in the pass.
The lord Yvain sprang to attack
the crowd. All of his strength was back
from his long rest. He struck a knight

2970 upon the shield with all his might.
The war horse and the rider fell
down in a great heap, so they tell,
and that knight never rose again,
because his backbone broke in twain,
and his heart burst within his chest.

The lord Yvain drew back to rest
a moment, then he seized his shield
and rushed onto the battlefield,
to clear the pass. Some time before
you could count one, two, three, and four,   2980
you'd have seen Sir Yvain, that day,
strike down four knights, and people say
the men with him began to gain
great courage from the lord Yvain,
because a man of timid heart
who sees a braver fighter start
to do a risky piece of work
before his eyes will never shirk.
He will be overcome by shame,
which drives the weak heart from his frame   2990
and gives him in its place the bold
heart of a brave man, so I'm told.
The men grew braver in this way
in battle. Each one chose to stay
and hold his ground and did not cower.
The lady in the castle tower
watched from on high, and she could see
the battle for her property.
She saw that many a warring knight
fell killed or wounded in the fight.   3000
Both her men and her foes were found
stretched out upon the battleground,
but far more of her foes were slain
than her own men. The lord Yvain,
so courteous, brave, and excellent,
made all her enemies consent
to yield to him, and come and kneel,
just as the falcon does the teal.
The men and women in the castle
exclaimed as they observed the battle,   3010

[89]

"Oh, what a valiant warrior,
who makes his foes fall back before
his fierce attack! Just see him fly on
the men around him like a lion
among the fallow deer when
his hunger goads him on! Our men
are braver for him. It's well known,
that were it not for him alone,
no lance would splinter, no sword would
3020   be drawn to strike. A good man should
be loved and cherished when he's found.
Just see the way he holds his ground
within the ranks! See him remain
the finest fighter! See him stain
with blood his naked sword and lance!
See how they move! See him advance
and press his foes into a mass!
See him ride toward them! See him pass
them by, as if he would give way,
3030   then see him turn! The knight, I'd say,
spends a few moments pulling back
and much time turning to attack!
Just see the way he fights! He cares
so little for his shield, he dares
to let his shield be cut away
without regret! The knight will pay
back with great pleasure all the blows
that he has gotten from his foes!
If all the trees within Argonne
3040   were felled to make him lances, none
would have remained by evenfall,
because the knight has broken all
the wooden shafts our men could store
in his lance rest and shouts for more!
See with what skill he strikes about

[90]

with his sword when he draws it out!
No, Roland never wrought such works
with Durendal against the Turks
at Roncesvalles or in Spain.
The traitor of whom we complain   3050
would be so harried he'd retreat,
or stand his ground and taste defeat,
if this lord had a company
of men who were as brave as he."

They said the lady he adored
would be so lucky, for the lord
was powerful, and in a fight
stood out from others like the light
of torches next to candle flames,
in the same way the moonlight shames   3060
the starlight, and the sun the moon.
The lord Yvain won all hearts soon.
The women and the men could see
how well he fought and wished that he
were married to their lady and
could be the master of their land.

So they admired him, and they knew
that all they said of him was true.
When he attacked the enemy,
they drew back and began to flee.   3070
On their heels, Sir Yvain gave chase.
His comrades followed him apace,
for next to him his comrades all
felt safe, as if a thick, high wall,
made of hard stone, encircled them.
The chase went on until the men
who fled became too tired to stand.
The men pursuing slashed them, and

then disemboweled their steeds. It's said

3080   the living rolled upon the dead.

They fought each other viciously.

Meanwhile the count began to flee.

At once the lord Yvain, in haste,

began to follow him. He chased

Count Alier some time, until

he caught the count beside a hill,

a steep one near the entrance ways

of a fort of Count Alier's.

The count was stopped there, out of reach,

3090   and so he didn't make a speech;

he yielded to the lord Yvain,

who had him in his hands. In vain

the count might try; there was no way

to flee or feign or fight, for they

were man to man alone, and so

Count Alier vowed he would go

yield to the lady of Noríson,

and put himself within her prison,

and make peace on her terms. The lord

3100   Yvain received his naked sword,

disarmed his head, removed his shield,

and took his word that he would yield.

They honored Sir Yvain that day,

because he led Count Alier

before him, so that he could hand

him over to the lady, and

his enemies did not restrain

their glee. The count and Sir Yvain

had not yet reached the castle wall,

3110   but word had gone ahead, and all

within came out to meet them, and

the lady led them. By the hand

the lord held fast his prisoner,

and he presented him to her.
From that time on, Count Alier
would do her will and would obey
the lady's orders, since the lord
had pledged to her his word and sword,
by oaths and by his faith. He swore
he'd live at peace forevermore   3120
with her, and he would pay the cost
of all things she could prove she'd lost.
He'd build new houses in the town
in place of those that he'd pulled down.
When everything had been agreed,
according to her wish and need,
the lord Yvain asked leave to go,
which she would not have given, though,
if he'd have stayed there all his life
with her his mistress or his wife.   3130
The lord Yvain would not accept
an escort for one step. He kept
his word and left in haste. In vain
would they have asked him to remain.
He went on back along the path
and left the lady full of wrath
to whom he'd given happiness,
because she was in worse distress,
despite the joy she'd felt that day,
when she learned that he would not stay.   3140
She wished to do him honor, and
to make him master of her land
and all she owned, if he desired,
or pay whatever he required
for helping her, however dear.
But he no longer wished to hear
another word from any man
or woman. Turning, he began

[93]

3150

to leave the knights and lady, though
it caused them such distress and woe
that they implored him to remain
more time with them, but all in vain.

YVAIN'S MEETING WITH THE LION

THE lord Yvain rode pensively
on through the deep wood. Suddenly
he heard an awful cry of pain
come from the trees. The lord Yvain
turned his horse and began to try
to find the place he'd heard the cry.
Within a clearing was a snake,

3160

which held a lion's tail, to rake
the lion's haunches with hot flame
and sear his flesh. The lord Yvain
did not watch long, though he delayed
while wondering which of them to aid.
But he decided he would go
and help the lion, for a low,
deceitful, deadly thing, with reason
may be harmed, and so full of treason
and poison is the snake, a flame

3170

leaps from its mouth. The lord Yvain
decided he would kill the snake.
He drew his sword, began to take
steps forward, and held up his arm
and shield, so hot flames would not harm
his face. The snake's throat belched forth hot
fire and was wider than a pot.
Now, if the lion should attack,
the lord Yvain would have no lack

of fights that day! But at the worst,
he planned to help the lion first,   3180
for pity pleaded with the knight
to help the lion in his plight,
the noble beast. He drew his sword—
its blade was keen—and then the lord
Yvain attacked the lowly snake
and cut him down, so he could break
the snake in two. Then Sir Yvain
struck at the snake time and again,
until the snake was cut in pieces.
But the dead snake would not release his   3190
head, which held the lion tight
and gripped him by the tail. The knight
was forced to cut away a bit
of the lion's tail to sever it.
So he cut off the least that he
could cut and set the lion free.
Then he was sure he'd have to fight
the lion, that the lion might
attempt to spring at him, but no,
the lion never would do so.   3200
I'll tell you what the lion then did,
because he was so brave and splendid:
the lion tried to make it plain
he yielded to the lord Yvain.
The lion rose on his hind feet
and joined his forepaws in complete
submissiveness, and then he spread
his forepaws out and bowed his head
in great humility. His face
was wet with tears. He knelt. His grace   3210
the lord Yvain most surely knew
the lion, very humbly too,
was thanking him because he'd saved

the lion's life when he had braved
and killed the wicked snake. The lord
Yvain was pleased. He cleaned his sword
of the snake's filthy poison, placed
it in the scabbard, and in haste
went on his way. The lion strode
3220 by Sir Yvain along the road
and never left the knight again.
He would go with the lord Yvain
forever, so he could protect
and serve him. Soon he could detect
the scent of grazing beasts upon
the wind, because the lion'd gone
ahead. His hunger and his will
urged him to hunt for them, and kill
and eat his prey for nourishment,
3230 and this would be what Nature meant
for him. Instead, he chose to go
on down the trail a bit to show
his master he had caught the scent
of animals. The lion went
ahead, and stopped, and looked at him,
prepared to serve his master's whim.
He did not want to disobey
his master in the slightest way.
In this way, Sir Yvain could know
3240 the lion did this deed to show
he'd wait to find out what to do
from Sir Yvain, who surely knew
if he stood still, the lion would wait,
but if he should so indicate,
the lion would run to catch the game
he'd scented. Sir Yvain, the same
as if the lion were a hound,
called out to him, and at the sound

[96]

he traced the scent he had perceived
and found he had not been deceived,   3250
because the lion had not gone
past bow's range, when he came upon
a roebuck grazing all alone
within a clearing. As he's shown,
the lion will seize the deer he's found,
and so he did, on the first bound,
and drank its warm blood. When the lion
had killed the deer, he laid it high on
his back, and brought the deer he'd slain
back to his master. Sir Yvain   3260
esteemed the lion all the more
for the great love the lion bore.

He wished to spend the evening there,
since night was falling, and prepare
and carve away as much red meat
from the deer as he wished to eat.
He split the skin so he could take,
beneath the ribs, a good loin steak.
He used his flint to strike a spark
and caught it in dry brush and bark.   3270
He put the steak upon a spit
close to the fire and roasted it
until it was cooked thoroughly.
But he did not enjoy it, he
possessed no bread, no knife, no fine
clean tablecloth, no salt, no wine.
But while he ate the roasted meat,
the lion lay still at his feet
and watched him steadily, until
his master had consumed his fill   3280
of the fat steak. When he was done,
the lion ate the venison,

[97]

down to the bare bones of his prey.
The lord Yvain, the whole night, lay
with head on shield, so that he could
obtain some rest within the wood.
The lion had so much good sense,
he stayed awake; with diligence
he watched the horse, which for some slight
3290   nutrition, grazed on grass all night.

At dawn they rose and went ahead
together, and I think they led,
for two more weeks, the life that they
had led there at the close of day,
until their fortune chose to bring
the pair back to the pine and spring.
Alas, that day the lord Yvain
believed he'd lose his mind again.
He saw the fountain and the stone.
3300   Since there was no way to atone
for his crime, he was miserable
and in such pain he swooned and fell.
His sword dropped from the scabbard, split
his hauberk's mail, and cut through it
beside the cheek and at the neck.
There is no mesh too strong to wreck,
and so the sharp sword did not fail
to cut the skin beneath the mail
beside the lord Yvain's neck, so
3310   it made his blood begin to flow.
The lion thought his comrade and
his lord lay slain by his own hand,
and you will nevermore be told,
nor hear narrated, nor behold
at any time, such grief and woe
as that the lion tried to show.

[98]

He cast himself about, and cried,
and clawed himself, and then he tried
to kill himself with the same sword
with which he felt sure that the lord   3320
Yvain had killed himself from grief.
He picked the sword up in his teeth,
and laid it on a fallen tree,
and propped the sword up carefully
against another tree trunk, lest
it slip back when he hurled his breast
against it. He'd almost obtained
his death wish, when his master gained
his senses back, and then the lion
restrained himself. He'd meant to fly on   3330
toward death like a wild boar; no pain
could change his mind. The lord Yvain
had fainted and was lying prone
in this way by the fountain's stone.
When he came to, in a short while,
at once he started to revile
himself for having been so late
and having earned his lady's hate.

"Who'd choose to suffer on alive
once he had managed to deprive   3340
himself of happiness forever?
Why do I live? How can I ever
stay here and see her vast domain?
Why should a soul choose to remain
in such a wretched body? Why
does my soul choose to stay in my
own body? For if it went free,
it would not live in agony.
I should despise and hate and blame
myself, and feel the greatest shame,   3350

[99]

for he who let his faults destroy
such happiness and such great joy
should hate himself so much he tried
to find some form of suicide;
and since nobody sees me, why
do I not kill myself? For I
have seen this lion was so sad
because of me, he almost had
succeeded and run my sword clear
3360 through his chest, so why should I fear
my own death, now I've had to change
my happiness for grief? How strange
all joy and gladness seem to me!
I'll say no more, for nobody
could talk about it; why employ
my time with foolish words? The joy
of which I was so sure, I call
the greatest happiness of all;
however it did not last long,
3370 and he who's lost such joy is wrong,
if it were by his faults and crimes,
to claim a right to better times."

LUNETTE CONDEMNED TO THE STAKE

BUT while the lord Yvain bemoaned
his sorry fate, complained, and groaned,
a maiden in the church, who had
been locked in, and was very sad,
was watching him, and heard it all
through a small crack within the wall.
As soon as he had come about,
3380 the maiden started calling out,

"Who's making all that noise outside?
Whom do I see there?" He replied,
"And who are you?" "The most ill-fated,
unhappy wretch alive," she stated.
He said, "Oh, hush, you silly thing!
What can you know of suffering?
Your grief is goodness, your woe glee,
compared with my great misery!
The more accustomed someone is
to living with delight and bliss,   3390
the more downcast and hurt is he
by woe than other men would be.
The weak man bears a burden longer
with years of practice than a stronger
man could bear the same load." "I see,"
the maid said, "but I disagree.
I know that what you say is true,
but still, I hardly think that you
have had to bear a greater woe
than I have. No, I don't think so,   3400
because it does appear to me
you go where you please and are free;
I am imprisoned. I can state
that I'll have such a dreadful fate,
tomorrow I'll be judged and sent
on to my death for punishment."
He said, "Oh, God, what have you done?"
"I hope God has no mercy, none,
upon my soul, if He can say
I earned this death in any way!   3410
But nonetheless, I will reply
and tell the truth; I do not lie.
I am a prisoner for this reason:
I'm charged with treachery and treason.
I've no defender, to my sorrow,

so I'll be burned or hanged tomorrow."
"Well, in the first place, I may say
that my own grief and my dismay
are worse than yours. Some knight may come

3420   here even now and save you from
your punishment. Is that not true?"
"Yes, sir, but I do not know who,
because I only know two knights
who would come to this place and fight
three men for my sake." "My God, three?"
"Yes, who charge me with treachery."
"And who are these two knights who hold
your life so dear, both would be bold
enough to fight three men to serve

3430   your cause in combat and preserve
your life, mademoiselle?" "Sir, I
will tell you, and this is no lie:
the first knight is the lord Gawain;
the second is the lord Yvain,
because of whom I shall be sent
tomorrow to my punishment,
and die unjustly in great pain."
"Who did you say he was?" "Yvain.
He's the son of King Urien."

3440   "Oh, now I see. I promise, then,
you will not die unless he does.
I am that same Yvain, because
of whom you are in such distress,
and you must be the maid, I guess,
inside the hall, who in the strife
preserved my body and my life
between the sliding doors the day
that I was in such great dismay,
and so upset her men had caught me.

3450   They would have captured me and brought me

to my death, were it not for you.
So now, my sweet friend, tell me who
charged you with treason, and as well
has shut you in this prison cell."

"Sir, I will hold back nothing, for
you say to tell it all. Before
I wanted, truly, to be nice
when I helped you. By my advice
my lady married you, and by
the holy paternoster, I   3460
thought and still think that it's been shown
more to her profit than your own.
I did it for your happiness
and for her honor, I confess.
So help me God, all this is true.
But later, when it happened you
forgot and overstayed the year
in which you'd promised to appear
before my lady, she became
so angry she began to blame   3470
and scold me, thinking I'd deceived her.
Of course the seneschal perceived her
resentment; he's a rascal who
has envied me, because he knew
full well in many matters she
did not trust him as much as me.
The seneschal knew that he might
find some way now to make us fight.
When everyone at court could hear,
he called me treacherous. I fear   3480
I had no one to counsel me,
so I replied too hastily
that I had never thought of one
deceitful deed and never done

[103]

harm to my lady. Sir, I cried
like a madwoman and replied
I'd be defended by a knight
who was so strong that he could fight
three men! I spoke without advice.

3490 The seneschal was not so nice
or courteous that he'd refuse,
and at that time I could not choose
to take back what the court had heard,
and so he took me at my word.
I furnished bail. In thirty days
I would present a knight who'd raise
his lance and sword against three men.
I've been at many courts since then,
and at King Arthur's court as well.

3500 I found no help. No one could tell
one word about you or knew where
you were. They'd no news of you there."

"That's true," replied the lord Yvain,
"but where was noble lord Gawain?
Because he's never failed to aid
a troubled and bewildered maid."
"I would have been extremely glad
and joyful if I only had
found him at court, because I could

3510 have asked for nothing that he would
refuse to give to me. But they
told me a knight, the other day,
had carried off the queen. The king
must have been mad, considering
he made her follow him with Kay.
The knight stole Arthur's queen away
from Kay. Then Sir Gawain departed
to try to find her, brokenhearted.

He will not take a day of rest
until he has fulfilled his quest. 3520
Now I have told you how my sorrow
has come about. Know that tomorrow
I shall be burned alive and make
a shameful death, burned at the stake
because of your forgetfulness."
The lord Yvain replied, "Unless
it pleases God, you will not be
burned at the stake because of me.
If I can help it, you won't die!
Tomorrow look for me, for I 3530
am well prepared to the extent
of all my forces to present
myself here and deliver you,
as it is fitting that I do.
But don't you dare tell any knight
who I am. Either way the fight
turns out, take care that nobody
around here recognizes me."
"No kind of pain could ever force
me to reveal your name, of course, 3540
because you do not wish me to
disclose it. Yet, I beg of you,
do not come back here for my sake.
I would not have you undertake
a fight so wicked and unfair.
Thank you for promising you'd dare
to fight the three knights for my cause.
But now you are released, because
it's better that I meet my fate
alone than see them celebrate 3550
your death and mine upon that day.
They would not let me go when they
had killed you. Better you remain

alive than both of us be slain."
"Fair friend, that's such a bad reply!"
the lord Yvain exclaimed. "Now I
suppose you don't care to be torn
from painful death, or else you scorn
the help and comfort that I bear!
3560   I won't say more of this affair;
as you have done so much for me,
I will not fail you, certainly,
when you need me! But, nonetheless,
I know you are in great distress.
Yet if God please, whose faith I claim,
the three knights will be brought to shame.
Mademoiselle, I have to go
and search for shelter, as I know
of no place to lodge in this wood."
3570   "Sir knight, may God give you a good
safe place to stay, and a good night
and guard you from all things that might
do harm to you," the maiden said.
He said good-bye and went ahead.
The lion followed as he rode.

HARPIN OF THE MOUNTAIN

THEY reached a baron's fine abode,
a castle well enclosed on all
four sides by a strong, thick, high wall.
The men inside feared no assault
3580   by mangonel or catapult,
for it was very strong. But near
the wall, outside, the land was clear
without a hut or house nearby,

[106]

and you will learn the reason why
another time, when there is space.
The lord Yvain went toward the place
along the fastest, shortest way,
and seven squires rose straightaway,
let down the bridge, and went outside
to him. The lion terrified   3590
the squires, who asked the lord Yvain
if he would make his lion remain
outside the castle gate, lest they
be killed or hurt. He answered, "Say
no more. I won't leave him behind,
and either both of us will find
our lodging place where you reside,
or else I will remain outside.
I love him like my own self, and
I will keep him so well in hand,   3600
you need not be afraid he'll stir."
The seven squires said, "Come in, sir."

They crossed onto the castle ground
and went ahead until they found
fair ladies, knights, and men-at-arms,
and lovely maids with many charms,
who came to greet them, and to aid him
remove his armor, and they bade him
be welcome to their house that day.
"We pray that God will let you stay   3610
as long as you can." High and low,
they strove to honor him and show
they welcomed him with joy. Apace
they led him to his lodging place
and welcomed Sir Yvain with gladness.
Then they were overwhelmed by sadness.
The people cried out in distress,

forgetting their great happiness,
and clawed themselves, and began to weep.

3620   For a long time they could not keep
from alternating joy and woe.
Their joy was for their guest's sake, though
in truth the people felt dismay
at what would happen the next day
by noon. It stunned the lord Yvain
that their mood changed, and changed again,
and mingled happiness with woe.
He told his host he'd like to know
the reason, if he would explain.

3630   "My God, sir," said the lord Yvain,
"Would you please tell me why you tried
to welcome me with joy, then cried?"
"Yes, if you want to know; however
you should want me to hide it. Never
of my own free will, will I say
what could but cause you great dismay.
Let us express our grief apart,
and please do not take it to heart."
"Sir, I could never see you make

3640   such lamentation and not take
your grief to heart, so let me know
the truth, no matter what great woe
it makes me feel." The lord said, "Then
I'll tell you that a giant's been
attacking me and caused this strife.
He sought my daughter as his wife,
because in beauty she excels
all other earthly demoiselles.
This wicked, evil giant, whom

3650   I pray that God confound and doom,
is Harpin of the Mountain. I
can tell you that no day's passed by

[108]

in which he has not stolen each
of my possessions he can reach.
No one is better justified
than I am to have mourned and cried.
I think my sorrow may unfix
my reason, sir, for I had six
fine sons, the handsomest and best
the world has ever seen, fair guest,   3660
six fine sons, all knights, and one day
the giant took all six away.
He has killed two of them before
my eyes; he'll kill the other four
tomorrow, if I find no knight
to save my sons from him and fight,
or else I shall be forced to yield
my daughter to him. He's revealed
he means to make her be the sport
of the most vile and oldest sort   3670
of groom and lackey in his house.
Now he won't take her as his spouse.
God help me, he will come tomorrow,
so do not wonder at our sorrow.
And yet, my lord, we've tried to make
our faces joyful for your sake.
A fool he who brings gentlemen
to be guests in his house, and then
won't honor them. You seem to be
a man of noble birth to me;   3680
and now, my lord, I find I've come
to telling you the total sum
of our misfortunes. Look around
outside upon the castle ground;
the giant's stripped it bare, except
for what we've brought in here and kept.
If you took notice, you would find

[109]

he has not left enough behind
to buy an egg. We have no more
3690　　than these new walls around us, for
the giant has razed the entire
town to the ground and then set fire
to what he left, so I can claim
that he has played a wicked game."
The lord Yvain weighed every word
his host had spoken. When he'd heard
it all, he said, "I'm very sad
and angry at the loss you've had.
Be sure I'm sharing your distress.
3700　　But there's one thing I cannot guess,
which is why you did not resort
to seeking counsel at the court
of good King Arthur. No man's might
is so great, there would be no knight
at Arthur's court who'd want to test
his strength and see which one is best."

At once the worthy man explained.
He showed that he could have obtained
great help and counsel in his plight
3710　　if he had but known where he might
have gone to find the lord Gawain.
"I'd not have sought his help in vain;
my wife is Gawain's sister. Still
a knight from a strange land, at will,
led off the queen, and they report
he came to seek her at the court.
He'd not have taken her away
so easily, except for Kay,
who tricked the king, so he directed
3720　　the queen to leave the court protected
by Kay alone. The more fool he,

[110]

and she behaved imprudently
as well, by choosing to entrust
herself to Kay. That's why I must
endure great loss and harm. My word,
if he had known what has occurred,
I know brave lord Gawain would cease
his quest and run to help his niece
and nephews, but he does not know.
I fear my heart may break from woe,   3730
for Sir Gawain has gone to fight
in foreign lands against the knight
whom God should punish and demean
for having led away the queen."
While listening, the lord Yvain
felt such grief he could not restrain
his sighs. "My lord," was his reply,
"I'll risk the danger, and I'll try
to fight the giant, to be sure,
provided that he comes with your   3740
four sons so early in the day,
it doesn't cause me much delay,
because I've promised to appear
at noontime somewhere else than here
tomorrow." The good man said, "I'm
in debt to you a thousand times
for what you've said you'll try to do."
The people in the castle, too,
agreed with him and said the same.
From a small room a maiden came.   3750
She had a figure full of grace,
a beautiful and pleasant face,
and yet she looked extremely sad
and quiet, for her sorrow had
no limit. She walked with her head
bowed low with suffering and dread.

[111]

Her mother came in by her side,
because the lord had notified
the two to come and see his guest.
3760 They came wrapped in their mantles lest
the tears that they were weeping show.
He ordered each of them to throw
her mantle back and raise her head.
"You should not hesitate," he said,
"for God and greatest luck have sent
a splendid man, who will consent
to fight against the giant; so
he has assured me. Hurry, throw
yourselves at his feet; don't delay!"
3770 "God never let me see the day,"
at once replied the lord Yvain,
"the sister of the lord Gawain
or his niece kneels down at my feet!
It is not right, and I entreat
the Lord to keep me fortified
against so great a sin of pride
as letting them fall down and kneel.
I'd never forget the shame I'd feel.
I wish they'd set aside their sorrow
3780 and be consoled until tomorrow,
when they'll see if God will provide
help and assistance for them. I'd
prefer not to be asked for more.
Let's hope the giant comes before
I have to leave for my affair,
so I won't break my word elsewhere,
because I will not fail to be
tomorrow by noontime at the
most urgent enterprise I know
3790 that I could ever have." And so
he did not want to reassure

them wholly. He could not be sure
the giant would arrive there soon
enough so he'd be back by noon
to help the maiden worrying
inside the chapel by the spring.
But nonetheless, the lord Yvain
began to give them hope again,
and everybody thanked him, since
they felt such hope and confidence.   3800
They knew how noble he must be;
his lion kept him company
and lay as gently by his side
as any lamb. Much fortified
by their hope in the lord Yvain,
they were consoled and glad again,
and wept no more in grief and woe.
When it was time, they had him go
into a spacious room to bed.
The maiden and her mother led   3810
the way; they'd honored him before,
and they would have done even more
for Sir Yvain, if they had known
the courtesy and strength he'd shown.
The lord Yvain and lion lay
and took their rest. No one dared stay
with them. Indeed, they locked the knight
and lion in the room all night.
The two could not get out before
dawn, when they opened up the door.   3820
The lord Yvain arose and heard
the Mass. So he would keep his word,
he stayed until the hour of Prime.
He called the lord in at that time
and said, "I have no more time now
to wait, sir, so you must allow

me to depart. I have to go;
I can't wait any longer, though
I wish so much I could, except
3830   I've made a pledge which must be kept
in some place very far away.
But otherwise, I'd surely stay
and help the niece and nephews of
the lord Gawain, a friend I love."

At this the lady and the maid
and gentleman were so afraid,
that every stomach, every heart
trembled with fear he might depart.
They wanted once again to throw
3840   themselves down at his feet, although
there was no chance of his permitting
a gesture that was so unfitting.
The lord attempted to propose
to give his guest whatever he chose
of his possessions or his land
to wait a little longer, and
the knight said, "God forbid that I
take any payment!" in reply.

The maiden, who was terrified,
3850   began to weep aloud. She cried
and came to Sir Yvain distraught
and tortured; she implored and sought
by the Lord God, the Seraphim,
and Heaven's Queen, entreating him
to wait. She begged the lord Yvain
not to go on, but to remain
for the sake of her uncle, too,
whom Sir Yvain had said he knew
and held in admiration. Then

great pity overwhelmed him, when   3860
he heard her pleading in the name
of the best friend that he could claim,
of Heaven's Queen, and of the One; He
who is compassion's sweet and honey.
In greatest woe, the lord Yvain
sighed deeply. Not for the domain
of Tarsus did the knight desire
to let the maiden die by fire
he'd vowed to help. The lord Yvain
would kill himself or go insane,   3870
were he too late to save her, and
he tarried, on the other hand,
because he felt such great distress
when he thought of the nobleness
of his good friend the lord Gawain.
The thought that he could not remain
was heartbreaking, and so he stayed,
and did not move on, and delayed,
until the giant brought the four
knights. He arrived in haste and wore   3880
around his neck a pointed stake,
big, square, and very sharp, to take
jabs at them. The knights' clothes, they saw,
were filthy shirts, not worth a straw,
and they could see the four knights' hands
and feet were tightly bound with strands
of cord. The knights rode up on four
poor, limping nags, thin, weak, and sore.
As ugly as a puffed-up toad,
a dwarf came with them as they rode.   3890
He'd tied the horses' tails up tight
together, and he beat each knight
with a six-knot whip till he bled,
to show how brave he was. They led

[115]

the four knights in disgrace and shame
between them. Dwarf and giant came
out of the woods and stopped beside
the main gate, where the giant cried
to the lord that he meant to slaughter
3900   his sons, unless he got his daughter,
and it would please the giant well
to give the gentle demoiselle
to all his lackeys as a whore,
since he no longer loved her or
esteemed her, and he would not deign
to marry her. But in his train
he had a thousand filthy men:
tramps, lackeys, scullions. All of them
were rogues and scoundrels, coarse and lewd,
3910   alive with lice, and mostly nude,
and would lay hands on her in turn.
The lord all but went mad to learn
his daughter would be made a whore,
or else, before his eyes, his four
sons would be killed. His agony
was that of one who'd rather be
dead than alive. The baron cried,
and mourned his sorry fate, and sighed.
Then noble lord Yvain began
3920   to say, like a straightforward man,
"My lord, that giant likes to boast
out in that clearing with his host.
He's very vile and impudent.
The Lord God never will consent
to let him have your daughter! He
insults and hates her. It would be
too awful to leave anyone
so very beautiful, and young,
and of such noble birth, to be

[116]

abandoned to his knaves. Bring me   3930
my horse and sword and armor too!
Lower the bridge and let me through!
For one of us will be brought low;
who it will be, I do not know,
but if I could humiliate
this man whose cruelty is so great,
so that he would be forced to free
your sons, and for the insults he
has spoken here, to make you just
amends, then, sir, I would entrust   3940
you to the Lord and go about
my business." Then the men led out
his horse, and brought his arms, and dressed
the lord Yvain. I can attest
that he was well equipped, and they
made no unnecessary delay!
They dropped the bridge, and off he went.
The lion, though, would not consent
to wait there. Everyone who'd stayed
behind thought of the knight and prayed   3950
to Saviour Christ, from dread and fear
the Devil might be drawing near.
He'd slaughtered many a brave knight
before their eyes, and he well might
kill Sir Yvain too. With one breath
they prayed, "God, save the knight from death,
and grant that he will kill his foe
and come back here alive," and so
each person softly prayed, inspired
according to what he desired.   3960
But at that time the giant bold
came toward the lord Yvain and told
the knight, "Upon my eyes, he who
has sent you here did not love you!

He couldn't find a better way
to take revenge on you! I say,
he has discovered a sublime
way to repay you for your crime!"
"You've started quarreling in vain,"
at once replied the lord Yvain,
who was not frightened, "Do your best,
and I will do mine, but a test
of idle chatter wearies me."

The lord Yvain raced at him; he
was anxious to be leaving, lest
he be late. He aimed at his chest,
which was protected by the hide
of a bear. On the other side,
the giant ran up with his stake.
The lord Yvain struck home to break
the chest skin with so hard a blow,
the giant's blood began to flow,
and wet the lance, like sauce for meat,
upon the iron tip. He beat
the lord Yvain hard with the stake,
until he'd struck enough to make
his foe bend down flat. Then the lord
Yvain reached out and drew his sword
to strike hard blows, for he could wield
it well. The giant had no shield,
for he had trusted in his might
and wore no armor. Then the knight,
whose sword was in his hand, applied,
with the sharp edge, not the flat side,
such a terrific blow with it,
he cut away a thick slice fit
for steak from his foe's cheek and head.
The giant struck a blow so dread,

3970

3980

3990

it nearly crushed the lord Yvain.
He sank down on his horse's mane. 4000

The lion bristled at this blow.
He wished to help his master, so
he sprang in rage, and struck, and tore
the thick bear's hide the giant wore
like so much bark, and underneath,
the lion tore off with his teeth
a great piece from the thigh and rent
the nerves and flesh. The giant went
away and bellowed like a bull.
His injury was terrible. 4010
He raised his stake high with both fists
to strike the lion, but he missed.
The lion leapt aside, and so
it was the giant missed his blow.
Then he collapsed and crouched, in pain,
exhausted, by the lord Yvain,
but did not touch him. Then the lord
Yvain took aim, and with his sword
slipped in two blows before his foe
recovered from the lion's blow. 4020
He cut his shoulder from his chest,
and then he struck beneath the breast
and through the liver. At this touch
the giant fell in death's firm clutch.
If a great oak fell to the ground,
there would not be a louder sound
than the noise of the giant's fall,
and everybody on the wall
tried very hard to see the blow.
It was made clear which men could go 4030
the fastest, for then everyone
came for the hunt's spoils on the run,

like hounds who've chased an animal
until they've killed it. So they all,
both men and women, did not stay;
they ran to where the giant lay
face downward, and the nobleman,
the mother, and the daughter ran,
and everybody at court, too.

4040   The brothers were so happy, who
had had to suffer so much pain.
They realized they could not detain
the lord Yvain a moment more,
so everyone tried to implore
the lord to come back there, and stay,
and celebrate upon the day
that he concluded his affair.
He answered that he did not dare
give them his word, because he could

4050   not know the outcome, bad or good,
but he had one request to make:
that the lord's sons and daughter take
the dwarf and find the lord Gawain,
when they learned he was back again,
because he wanted them to say
how well he had behaved that day,
for he who wishes to conceal
his noble deeds must really feel
they have no value. They replied,

4060   "Of course it is not right to hide
such kindness, and we'll gladly go
to Sir Gawain. But may we know
whom we shall honor and acclaim,
because we do not know your name?"

He answered, "This much you may say,
when you have come to him that day:

[120]

tell him I told you that you might
address me by the name of "the Knight
with the Lion." I ask you to tell
the lord Gawain he knows me well,   4070
and I know him well too, although
he's never heard this name. And so
I ask no more, for I must be
upon my way immediately,
and I am very much afraid
that by now, I may well have stayed
too long, for by noon I've a plan
to do much elsewhere, if I can
arrive in time." He rode away
without a moment of delay.   4080
The nobleman tried to implore
the lord Yvain to take his four
sons with him. Any one of those
men there would serve him, if he chose.
It did not suit the lord Yvain
that any one of them remain
with him or keep him company.
He left them far behind, and he
rode off alone upon his steed.

LUNETTE'S RESCUE

HE galloped on at breakneck speed   4090
back to the church. The path was good;
he knew the way, but before he could
get to the spring and end his ride,
the knights had dragged the maid outside
the church and had prepared the stake
and pyre upon which she would make

[121]

her end, clad just in her chemise.
The maiden was held bound by these
disloyal knights beside the fire,
4100   who claimed that she'd tried to conspire
against her lady. At no time
had she considered such a crime.
The lord Yvain arrived and learned
that she was ready to be burned.
The lord Yvain was furious,
and it would not be courteous
or wise to doubt it! But, despite
his rage, he thought that God and Right
would help him and be on his side.
4110   He had great faith, and he relied
upon God, nor did he disdain
his lion's help. The lord Yvain
rushed toward the crowd while shouting, "No!
You wicked people, let her go!
You have no right to try to take
the maid and burn her at the stake,
for she is innocent!" The mass
of people quickly let him pass.
He hoped that he would catch sight of
4120   the only lady he could love.
His heart saw her in every place
he went. His eyes searched for her face
and found it. Seeing her again
had put his heart to such great strain,
he had to hold his heart in check
and rein it in, as you subject
a restless horse to a strong rein
and find him awkward to restrain.
The lord Yvain was glad to look
4130   and see the lady, but he took
great care that he controlled his eyes

and let nobody hear his sighs.
With a great effort he restrained
his sighs. Then he was greatly pained
and seized by pity. He beheld
poor ladies whom their grief compelled
to make a curious lament.
He heard them say, "It's evident,
God, you've forgotten us. We'll find
ourselves quite lost without so kind   4140
a friend, so helpful, and so nice,
who gave us excellent advice
at court. She asked our lady fair
to clothe us in her robes of vair.
How things will change! Nobody can
speak for us now. Cursed be the man
who took her from us! Cursed be he
who charged Lunette with treachery!
because we shall fare badly; there
will be nobody to say, 'Fair,   4150
dear lady, give this robe, this hood,
this vest, this mantle, to this good
and honest woman. If you choose
to send them, I am sure she'll use
the clothes well, she needs them so much.'
No one will ever utter such
kind words or show such courtesy
again, or such sincerity.
Each one speaks for herself from greed,
although she may not be in need."   4160

The ladies grieved, and Sir Yvain,
who was with them, heard them complain
aloud, and certainly he knew
that their lament was real and true.
He saw Lunette upon her knees,

[123]

clad only in a light chemise.
She had confessed her sins in full,
and asked God to be merciful,
and beat her breast. The lord Yvain
4170   was so fond of Lunette, he came
and raised her up at once, and then
he said to her, "Where are the men,
fair maid, who wanted to accuse
and charge you? If they don't refuse,
I'm challenging them now to fight."
Lunette had not yet seen the knight.
She said, "You come from God indeed
to help me in this time of need!
The men who have accused me stand
4180   before me at this moment, and
I know that I would have become
hot coals and ashes if you'd come
much later! May the Lord agree
to strengthen you to the degree
that I'm not guilty of the crime
of which I am accused!" Meantime
the brothers and the seneschal
had overheard and told them all,
"Ha! Such is woman! With truth tight
4190   and lavish with her lies. The knight
is very foolish to agree
to such work on your guarantee!
How ill-advised is this knight who
came all this way to die for you,
for we are three and he's but one!
I think he'd better turn and run
before he's badly hurt or slain!"

They made him angry; Sir Yvain
said, "Anyone who's scared can flee!

I'm not so frightened by your three   4200
shields I'll make up my mind to go
away before I've struck one blow!
I'm not so simple I will yield
the fight to you and battlefield
while I am still unhurt and strong.
I'll never flee from threats as long
as I live with no injury!
But I advise you men to free
the maiden you've unjustly blamed,
for I believe her, and she's claimed   4210
in peril of her soul, and pledged
her word she never once alleged,
performed, or thought of any crime
against her lady, anytime.
Now I believe her, and I will
defend her cause, if possible,
because her rights are on my side.
He who speaks truth is justified,
for God sides with the Right alway,
and God and Right are one. If they   4220
are both on my side, I can be
assured of better company
and help than you." The seneschal
said to do anything at all
he could to harm them in the fray,
but make the lion keep away!
He'd said a very foolish thing.
The lord replied he'd never bring
his lion as his champion,
and he did not want anyone   4230
to come and help him out. But let
the three knights who'd accused Lunette
defend themselves as best they might,
in case the lion tried to fight,

because the lord Yvain said he
did not intend to guarantee
the lion would avoid the fray.

They said, "No matter what you say,
if you refuse to warn and chide
4240   your lion to keep to one side
and lie still, then you need not stay,
use common sense and go away,
for everybody in this land
knows that the demoiselle had planned
to wrong her lady and should claim
her due reward in fire and flame."
"The Holy Ghost will not allow
the maiden to be burned!" Her vow
he knew was true. "God, do not let
4250   me move from here until Lunette
has been saved!" said the lord Yvain
and told his lion to remain
behind the sidelines, and lie still.
The lion did his master's will.

The parley ended as the two
who spoke stepped backward and withdrew.
Each of the three knights spurred his steed:
the lord met them at walking speed.
He did not want to be upset
4260   or hurt by the first blow; he let
them split their lances; his shield served
as target for them. He preserved
his lance intact and rode around
to put an acre's space of ground
between them. After this delay
he turned and rode back to the fray.
He reached the seneschal, by chance,

[126]

before the rest, and broke his lance
upon him. Sir Yvain struck well,
so hard the seneschal then fell   4270
down to the ground, against his will,
and lay there stunned, incapable
for a long time of causing trouble.
The brothers fell on him, a double
assault with bared swords; each one dealt
the lord a crushing stroke, but felt
a harder stroke in turn—one blow
of his was worth two of theirs. So
the brothers fought with him and found
he fought so well, they gained no ground,   4280
until the seneschal arose
and did his best to land hard blows.
The brothers joined in, and the three
struck him and did him injury.
When they began to overcome
the knight, the lion, watching from
the sidelines, saw he needed aid
immediately. The ladies prayed
wholeheartedly, from their great love
for the maid, to the Lord above,   4290
not to allow the lord Yvain
to lose the battle or be slain,
because he fought to bring her aid.
The ladies helped with prayers, since they'd
no other sticks. The lion brought
such help, that at the first assault
the seneschal, back on his feet,
was hit so hard, the lion's teeth
had made the hauberk's meshes fly
away like straws, thin, light, and dry.   4300
He dragged him down with even more
ferociousness and struck and tore

[127]

the shoulder's flesh away, around
and down the side. All that he found
or touched, the lion stripped and scraped,
until the viscera escaped.
The other brothers, at the sight,
avenged this blow with all their might.
Then they were even on the field.

4310   The seneschal was forced to yield
to death. He weltered in the flood
of great waves of bright crimson blood
that poured out from his trunk and chest.
The lion turned and struck the rest.
The lord could not stop his attack,
though he tried hard to drive him back
by striking him and threatening too.
Undoubtedly the lion knew
his master did not hate him for

4320   his help, but loved him all the more,
so his attack was unrestrained.
He fought the two till they complained,
and then the brothers whirled around
and struck the lion to the ground.

Once that the lord Yvain could see
his lion wounded horribly,
the heart within his body burned.
Enraged, the lord Yvain returned
such hard blows in revenge, the two

4330   knights were so badly hurt, they threw
themselves upon his mercy, swayed
by terror of the lion's aid.
The lion lay in dreadful pain
with two bad wounds. The lord Yvain
was very far from being well,
for he had many wounds. They tell

[128]

the wounds did not hurt Sir Yvain
as much as did his lion's pain.
By then he'd set the maiden free.
Her lady pardoned her, and she   4340
would not be angry anymore.
The other men were brought before
the fire which they had lit to burn
the maiden, and were burned in turn,
for it is right and just that he
who charged another wrongfully
should die by the same death he'd set
for him he had accused. Lunette
was overjoyed to be, at last,
her lady's friend as in the past,   4350
and both of them rejoiced far more
than anybody had before.
The people present offered to
serve their own lord, though no one knew
he was Yvain, and even she
who had his heart unknowingly
came to the knight, and she appealed
to him to stay till he was healed.
He said, "My lady, I won't stay
in your domain until the day   4360
my lady's pardoned me and ceased
to be so angry and displeased.
Upon that day my trials will end."
"But this news saddens me, my friend.
I do not think the lady who
has anger in her heart for you
can be a courteous person, for
she is not right to close her door
against so fine a knight, unless
he caused her great woe and distress."   4370
"My lady, never mind what pain

[129]

I suffer," said the lord Yvain.
"I'm pleased by all she may desire
to do to me. But don't inquire;
I won't discuss the cause or crime
with anyone, except when I'm
with people who already knew
about it." "But besides you two,
does anyone know of the deed?"

4380   "My lady, yes, they do indeed."
"My lord, you will be free to go
when you've told us your name." "Free? No,
I'm sure I'll never see that day;
I owe far more than I can pay.
In any case, I won't try to
conceal or hide my name from you.
You'll never hear about the Knight
with the Lion, and not hear them cite
the name by which I wish to be

4390   known to all men who hear of me."
"For Heaven's sake, what does that mean?
I'm certain we have never seen
or heard of you before you came!"
"I've only lately made a name
for myself, my lady." As before
the lady said to him, "Once more,
if you did not seem so distressed,
I'd plead with you to stay and rest."
"My lady, that I would not do,

4400   most certainly, until I knew
that I possessed my lady's heart."
"In that case, sir, you may depart,
and go with God! May all your woe
and grief be turned to joy, if so
be His will!" "Lady," he said, "may
the Lord God hear you when you pray!"

[130]

And then he added quietly,
"My lady, you hold the lock and key
and casket where my happiness
is kept, and yet you cannot guess."   4410

Then he left her, in dreadful pain.
No one knew he was Sir Yvain
except Lunette alone. She rode
with him a long way down the road;
the only person in the town
who'd chosen to ride with him down
the road, and all the way the lord
Yvain beseeched her and implored
Lunette not to tell anyone
whom she'd had as her champion.   4420
She said, "My lord, I never will."
The lord Yvain implored her still
to think about him and impart
a good place in her lady's heart
for him, if such a chance arose.
Lunette said hush, did he suppose
that she would not keep him in mind,
or be so lazy and unkind?
He thanked her many times, and sought
for shelter, worried and distraught   4430
about his lion. Sir Yvain
was carrying him, for his pain
was so intense, the lion could
not walk behind him through the wood.
The knight made him a litter. Across
his shield he put some ferns and moss
to make the lion a soft bed.
He laid him down and went ahead.
The lion was stretched out inside
the shield and had an easy ride.   4440

[131]

The lord Yvain then rode along
and reached the front gate of a strong,
fine mansion. It was closed, so he
called out once, and immediately
the porter opened with such speed,
the lord Yvain had felt no need
to think of calling him again.
The porter took the horse's rein
in his hand. "Fair sir, go ahead.
4450   I offer my lord's house," he said,
"as lodging, if you will descend."
"And I accept your offer, friend.
It's time to find a lodging place,
which I need greatly in this case."
He rode on through the gate. In passing
he saw a group of men amassing
to welcome him into their town.
They helped the lord Yvain get down
and eased the shield, so it would lie on
4460   the courtyard's paving stones. The lion
lay in it, seriously disabled.
They made sure that the horse was stabled.
The squires came out and helped the knight
remove his armor, as was right.
When the lord heard, he came at once
to greet him outside, with his sons
and daughters, wife, and a whole crowd
of people, and the lord was proud
and pleased to have the knight reside
4470   in his house. They put him inside
a quiet room, for he was ill.
Although it tested their good will,
the people put the lion in
with him. Two maids, in medicine
well educated, and who were

the lord's daughters, began to cure
the lion and the knight. Now I
don't know how many days went by
until at last their wounds were gone,
and so they made themselves go on.   4480

THE LORD OF THE BLACK THORN'S DAUGHTERS

AT this same time the tales relate
the lord of the Black Thorn's debate
with Death. Death made him a reply
so crushing that he had to die.
When he was dead, the way things fared,
his elder daughter soon declared
that she would hold in her possession
all the lord's lands, without a question,
for all the days she had to live,
and furthermore, she'd never give   4490
her younger sister any part.
His younger daughter said she'd start
for good King Arthur's court, and there
she'd seek help to defend her share.
But when the elder saw, indeed,
her younger sister'd not concede
her rightful portion of the land
without a fight, she was vexed, and
she told her sister that she would
arrive at court first, if she could.   4500
She packed her bags without delay
and did not pause; she rode away
until she reached the court at last.
Her sister followed her as fast
as possible, but found her haste

[133]

and her long journey were a waste.
The elder'd had time to explain
her point of view to Sir Gawain,
and he had promised he would do
4510   whatever she might ask. The two
agreed, however, that no one
would learn about what they had done
from her, or else the lord Gawain
would not bear arms for her again.
The younger sister came to court
at that time, and she wore a short
silk cloak with ermine fur. They say
she came there three days past the day
that Arthur's queen returned home free
4520   from Meleagant's captivity.
By treachery and evil power,
Sir Lancelot was in the tower
a captive. Also, on the same
day that the younger sister came
to Arthur's court, there came as well
the news about the terrible
and cruel giant, whom the Knight
with the Lion slaughtered in the fight.
The lord Gawain's four nephews came
4530   and greeted him in the knight's name,
and his niece started to relate
the knight's vast courage and the great
and noble service he'd performed
on their behalf, and she informed
her uncle that he knew the knight
extremely well, although he might
not know him by that name. Each word
she spoke, the younger sister heard.
The maid was heartbroken, downcast,
4540   and desperate, because at last

[134]

she realized she would find no aid
and no advice at court. The maid
had lost the finest knight. They say
she had appealed in every way,
by love and prayer, to Sir Gawain,
but he'd replied, "My friend, in vain
do you beseech me and implore
that I fight when I cannot, for
at present I am occupied
with matters I won't put aside."   4550
The maiden left the lord Gawain
at once and went in to explain
before the king. "King," said the maid,
"I came to your court seeking aid,
but I've found none, and it's surprised me
that no one's helped me or advised me.
I'd be ill-mannered, I believe,
to go away without your leave.
My elder sister should have known
she could have had all that I own   4560
for love, if she had wished. I swear,
however, since she's been unfair,
that she will not force me to give
my portion to her while I live,
if I can find advice and aid."
"You're wise," King Arthur told the maid,
"so I shall urge and recommend her,
since she is present, to surrender
the land to which you have a right."
The elder, with the finest knight   4570
on earth, replied, "God strike me down,
Sire, if I yield one castle, town,
one clearing, forest, meadow, and
the smallest portion of my land
to her! If there are any knights

who'll bear arms to defend her rights,
let them step forward if they dare!"
The king said, "No, you are unfair.
She needs more time, and so she may
4580   seek help for two weeks from today
at least, according to the sort
of judgment used in every court."
The elder sister said, "Because,
fair lord King, you may make your laws
as you please, any way it might
seem good to you, and I've no right
to disagree, I must obey,
if she desires such a delay."

The younger sister said indeed
4590   she wished it so, and she would need
the time. She would commend the king
to God and would go traveling
in every land to seek the Knight
with the Lion, who did all he might
for women who had need of aid.
So it was in this way the maid
began her quest and rode about
in many different lands without
a word of news of him, until
4600   her sorrow made her very ill.
But good came of it in the end.
She'd reached the dwelling of a friend.
Her friend had always loved her dearly
and could see by her face that clearly
she was not well. So they detained
the maiden there till she explained
her business. Then, so she could rest,
another maid took up her quest.
The other maiden rode all day

[136]

alone along the narrow way   4610
in haste until the dark night fell.
But the night caused the demoiselle
much worry, and as if to double
the maiden's terror and her trouble,
before long it began to rain
with all the Lord God's might and main,
while she was in the woods. The night
and forest caused the maid great fright,
and what distressed her more again
than woods and darkness, was the rain.   4620
The road was so bad that her horse
sank to its girth in mud. Of course
a maid alone in blackest night
and rain deep in the forest might
indeed feel worried and afraid!
The night was so black, that the maid
found that she could not see the steed
on which she sat. So, in her need,
the maiden first began to call
on God, His Mother, then on all   4630
the saints, and prayed that God might end
her troubles, find her shelter, send
safe lodgings to her, so she could
take rest, and lead her from the wood.
The maid prayed on. To her delight
she heard a horn blow in the night.
She hoped to find a lodging place
within her reach. She turned to face
in the direction of the sound,
and came to a paved road, and found   4640
that the paved road, as she'd inferred,
would take her toward the sound she'd heard.
The horn had been blown loud and long
three times. The maiden rode along

[137]

and went straight on until she spied
a cross set up on the right side
of the road which she hoped would lead
her to the horn. She spurred her steed
along the road and traveled fast
4650 in that direction, till at last
she reached a bridge and was in sight
of a round castle which had white
walls and high ramparts. So she found
the place by chance and by the sound
of the horn, because the horn had caught
her ear, and in this way had brought
her to the castle gate alone.
A watchman on the walls had blown
the horn. As soon as he could see
4660 the maid, he came down with the key
to open up the gate. He bade
her enter, and he said, "Fair maid,
be welcome here, whoever you might
be, you'll have a good room tonight."
"I ask no more," the maid replied.
The watchman led the maid inside.
With all her trouble, and her great
exertion, she was fortunate
to have found lodgings there of some sort,
4670 and she was lodged in greatest comfort.
Much later, when her hosts had brought
her supper, they asked what she sought
and where she went. The maid began
to say, "I'm looking for a man
whom I believe I've never set
my eyes upon and never met,
but he is always with a lion,
and I've been told I can rely on

this knight, if I find him." "That's so,"
her host replied. "Two days ago   4680
the Lord God graciously agreed
to send him here in my dire need,
and blessings on the road that brought
the knight to my house, for he fought
here with a mortal enemy
of mine. He filled me full of glee
by taking vengeance in such wise,
he killed my foe before my eyes.
Tomorrow morning we should have her
go out and look at the cadaver   4690
of that huge giant. He expired
so fast, the knight scarcely perspired."
"Oh, Heavens," said the demoiselle,
"if you do know the truth, please tell
where the knight went; tell me which way,
and where he might decide to stay."
"As God's my witness, I don't know,"
he said. "Tomorrow I will show
the road to you by which he went."
The maiden said, "May God consent   4700
to lead me somewhere I will hear
real news of him. If I get near
and find him, my joy will be great."

So they talked on till it was late
and went to bed. But at the break
of day, she rose to overtake
the knight that she had tried to find.
The master of the house was kind.
He rose with all his men and showed
the maiden to the proper road   4710
to reach the spring and pine. She sped

[139]

straight on along the road that led
back to the lady's town, and then
the maid inquired of the first men
she met if they knew where she might
go, so that she could find the knight
who had a lion by his side
who fought with him. The men replied
they'd seen him conquer three knights, and
4720   upon that very strip of land.
The maiden started to appeal
at once. "Oh, Heavens, don't conceal
a single word; since you've said so
much, tell me everything you know."
"No," they replied, "we know no more
about it than we said before,
and we do not know what became
of him. If she for whom he came
and fought can tell you nothing new,
4730   then no one can enlighten you.
But you won't have to go elsewhere to
discuss it with her, if you care to:
she's gone inside that church to hear
the Mass and pray. It does appear
from all the time that she's been staying,
she should be nearly done with praying!"

Lunette came from the chapel then,
while they were talking, and the men
said, "There she is." The maiden met
4740   and greeted her. She asked Lunette
about the lion and the knight.
Lunette sent for her palfrey right
away, because she wished to make
part of the trip with her and take

her to the place where they had parted.
The maiden's "Thank you" was wholehearted.
The palfrey came without delay;
the ladies mounted and rode away.
Lunette began to tell how she
had been accused of treachery, 4750
and how they had prepared the pyre
on which she was to die by fire,
and how the knight came and agreed
to help her in her time of need.
While she was speaking, she took care
to lead the maid to the spot where
the lord Yvain left her, when she
had gone to keep him company.
She said, "Ride down this road until
you come to some place where you will 4760
hear more complete and better news,
if God and Holy Spirit choose.
I know I left him either near
this place or else exactly here.
We have not seen each other since,
and what he did when he went hence
I don't know, for I stayed behind.
I do know that he had to find
a doctor quickly. You can follow
his trail; by nightfall or tomorrow 4770
please God that you be reassured
and find him in good health and cured.
Now I commend you to God's care
as you go on. I do not dare
ride on and keep you company;
my lady might be cross with me."
Lunette left her and turned around.
The maid went on until she found

4780

the house where they had lodged the lord
Yvain until he was restored
to health, and she saw by the gate
the lord and ladies of the estate,
armed men, and knights. The demoiselle
addressed them, asking them to tell
all information that they might
have heard about a certain knight
she sought. "I've heard they say about
this knight, he's never seen without
a lion." The lord said, "I vow!

4790

Fair maid, that knight left us just now,
and you can reach him by tonight,
if you can keep his tracks in sight.
But careful, don't lose any time!"
"Sir, God forbid! Say which road I'm
to take to follow him," she said.
They told her, "This way, straight ahead."
They asked the maid to greet the knight
on their behalf, but their polite
request was useless, for the maid

4800

had galloped off and scarcely paid
attention to the people's talk.
Her palfrey's gait seemed like a walk.
She galloped through the mud and rode
as fast through mud as on smooth road,
until at last she saw the knight
whose lion came to help him fight.
"God help me now!" the maiden cried
in her great joy. "Now I have spied
the knight whom I've pursued, whose track

4810

I've followed so far, but alack!
If I can reach him; if I try it,
what if I do not profit by it,

if nothing's gained? My word, if he
refuses to go on with me,
then all my effort is a waste!"
But as she spoke, the maiden raced
after the knight so fast, her steed
was in a lather. Soon, though, she'd
been able to attain his side
and greet the knight, and he replied,　　　　　　4820
"God save you, lovely one, and so
preserve you from concern and woe!"

"The same to you! I hope," said she,
"that you'll be able to save me!"
The maid drew near and said, "I came
to seek you, sir, for your great fame
and prowess made me travel through
so many lands in search of you.
I'm so tired, but it does appear
I've searched enough to find you here,　　　　　　4830
thank God, and if I felt some pain
in coming here, I don't complain,
or care, or think of how I grieved;
I am so utterly relieved.
When I found you, my sorrow fled.
This is not my affair. Instead,
a better woman, valiant,
and nobler than I am, has sent
for you; she is in desperate need.
If you refuse to help, indeed,　　　　　　4840
your reputation has betrayed her,
for no one else will help or aid her,
except for you, sir, now that she
has lost all of her legacy
to her mean sister. So the maid

[143]

hopes to win justice with your aid.
She wants no one else; she believed
her purpose would not be achieved
by anybody else but you.
4850 You'd be more famous, it is true.
When you've fought for the landless one
and won her rights back, you'll have won
a finer reputation. She
was going to seek you personally
to ask you for this boon: to pledge
that you'd defend her heritage.
She'd have no one else come instead,
but she's been forced to stay in bed
and been detained by illness. So
4860 would you please answer yes or no;
if you will dare to come, or choose
instead to tell her you refuse?"

He said, "I don't refuse. I claim
a life of ease wins no man fame,
and so I promise to defend
her cause. I'll follow you, sweet friend,
most willingly to any land
you wish, and you must understand;
if she on whose behalf you sought
4870 my help has need of me, you ought
not to despair, because I vow
to do all I can do. And now
God grant me grace and strength that day,
so that, by His wisdom, I may
be able to make His Right reign."
The two began to ride again.

THEY talked until they had drawn near
the Castle of Evil Adventure. I fear
they'd no desire to pass it by,
because the night was drawing nigh.   4880
They rode up to the castle. All
who saw them come began to call,
"Ill come, Sir knight, ill come! This place
was meant to cause you shame, disgrace,
and make you suffer harm and pain;
an abbot'd swear so!" Sir Yvain
replied, "You stupid, common people,
so full of every kind of evil,
devoid of every quality,
why did you start attacking me?"   4890
"Why? Now, Sir knight, if you will go
a little further, you'll soon know!
But you'll learn nothing more at all,
unless you ride through that high wall!"
At once the lord Yvain turned to
the castle wall. They shouted, "Boo!
Where are you going, you poor man?
If ever in your life you ran
across someone who brought disgrace
on you, what they'll do in that place   4900
to hurt you will be so much worse,
you'll never live to tell." "Perverse
and stupid people, who disdain
all honor," said the lord Yvain
who heard them. "What's this? Why accuse
and blame me? Why do you abuse
and growl at me?" "They don't intend
to be rude; don't be cross, my friend,"

[145]

an aged lady told the knight,
4910 for she was prudent and polite.
"None of their words mean that they scorn you;
instead, these people want to warn you,
if you but knew, not to lodge there,
but none of them would ever dare
to tell you why. They scold, Sir knight,
because they're trying to ignite
your fears, and they have done the same
with all the other knights who came
to this town, so they'd not go there.
4920 This is our custom. We don't dare
give lodgings in our homes to strangers,
and so we warn them of the dangers.
No one is standing in your way;
you are your own man, and you may
go up there, if you so decide,
but I think you should turn aside."
"My lady," said the lord Yvain,
"if I did so, I ascertain
it would be wiser, and in fact
4930 might help keep my good name intact.
But I don't know where else I might
obtain a place to lodge tonight."
"Upon my word, I'll say no more,"
the lady said in answer, "for
you may go anywhere you please.
I know I'd feel much more at ease
if I saw you return from there
without too much disgrace to bear,
but I know that can never be."
4940 "May God reward you properly,"
said Sir Yvain. "But still my heart
is willful, and it tells me 'start

[146]

on toward that gate and go inside'
so I'll do what my heart decides."

He went to the gate, unafraid,
so did his lion and his maid.
The porter called to them and cried,
"Come quickly, for you have arrived
at such a place that you will be
securely kept, and cursed be   4950
your coming!" So the porter said
this nasty greeting, and he sped
on up the stairs. The lord Yvain
passed straight through, for he did not deign
to answer, and beyond the wall
he found a new and spacious hall.
In front of the great hall he found
a yard enclosed with long, sharp, round
stakes, and inside these barricades
he saw at least three hundred maids   4960
who worked at every different kind
of stitching, and each one entwined
her work with silk and golden thread
as best she knew. Their fingers sped.
The maids were so poor, many wore
no belts and were untidy, for
they'd worn holes in their clothes at breast
and elbow and were poorly dressed.
Their shifts were soiled, their necks were gaunt,
their faces pale and starved with want.   4970
He looked at them, and when they spied
the knight, they bent their heads and cried.
For some time they were so dismayed,
they could not work. No maiden raised
her eyes; because they felt such pain

and misery. The lord Yvain
watched them a while, turned, and went straight
back, but the porter barred the gate.
"No use, fair sir," the porter cried.

4980 "Now you would like to be outside,
but on my soul, I won't allow
your leaving or escaping now,
till you have suffered so much shame,
you could not suffer more. You came
into this castle foolishly,
and there's no way for you to flee!"
"Fair brother, that is not my goal.
But tell me, by your father's soul,
from what place came the maidens whom

4990 I saw when I went past that room?
They're weaving cloth of silk and gold,
embroidered finely to behold,
but they are much too thin and sad
and pale, and they are poorly clad,
although I think that they would be
quite elegant and fair to see,
if they had pretty things instead."
"I'll never tell," the porter said.
"Find someone else." "I will obey,

5000 because there is no better way."
The lord Yvain, by searching hard,
soon found the entrance to the yard
wherein the maidens stitched and sewed,
still hard at work, and so he strode
inside the yard to greet them all,
and he could see the teardrops fall
from their eyes as the maidens cried.
He said to them, "May God decide
to rid your hearts of this great woe;

5010 what causes it I do not know;

[148]

and turn it into joy." One maid
said, "Would God heard you when you prayed!
Who we girls are I will disclose,
and from what land, for I suppose
that's what you wanted to inquire."
"I did come here with that desire."

"Sir knight, it happened a long while
ago. The King of Maidens' Isle
went seeking news throughout all sorts
of lands and came to many courts,   5020
just like a simpleton, I fear.
At last he fell in danger here.
He came at an unlucky hour.
We wretched captives have to cower
and live in misery and shame,
though we are in no way to blame.
(Sir knight, be sure you can expect
a shameful fate if they reject
your ransom!) But at any rate,
the king arrived here at the gate.   5030
Within this castle there are two
sons of a devil (Sir knight, do
not think this is some tale I've gleaned!)
born of a woman and a fiend.
These demons were about to fight
the king. He felt tremendous fright,
because he was not yet eighteen
and knew the demons would cut clean
through his flesh like a tender lamb.
In terror, the young king began   5040
to save himself as best he could.
So, at that time, he swore he would
send thirty maidens and would give
more maids each year he had to live,

[149]

and with this promise he was freed.
This contract, he swore and agreed,
would last the demons' lifetimes through,
unless some knight could kill the two
in combat, and upon that day
5050   he would no longer have to pay
this tribute, and we would be free
from sorrow, shame, and misery.
But we won't have one thing we like
at any time; I'm speaking like
an infant when I talk about
our being saved. We won't get out,
we'll stay here all our lives to weave
this silken cloth, and I believe
we never will be better dressed.
5060   No, we will always be hard-pressed,
poor, hungry, thirsty, and bare, for
we earn too little to buy more
to eat. Our bread supply is tight:
a bit at morning, less at night,
since none of us is given more
each day to live upon than four-
pence for her handwork. I conclude
we'll always lack warm clothes and food,
though someone who each week earns twenty
5070   shillings should have bread aplenty!
And every maiden, you will learn,
weaves cloth enough each week to earn
that sum, and often more, with which
a duke would be considered rich!
This is the way we are reduced
to poverty: our master's used
to growing richer by our work.
We toil all day, and never shirk,
and sit up half the night. His men

have threatened us with torture when   5080
we've tried to rest, and so we do
not dare take rest. But why tell you
about it? We are being used
so badly and are so abused,
that I can't even undertake
to tell a fifth of it. We shake
with anger every time that we
are forced to sit here and to see
a gentleman or some young knight
be killed because he had to fight   5090
with the two devils. Dearly do
they pay to lodge here, and so you
will do tomorrow, when you'll be
forced, at will or unwillingly,
to fight the two alone and shame
your reputation and your fame."
"May God, our true and spiritual
King keep me safe and let you all
have joy and honor once again,
if He will," said the lord Yvain.   5100
"Now I must go inside and see
about their hospitality."
"Go now, Sir knight, and we implore
Him who gives all good from His store
to keep you safely." Then he ventured
around the castle till he entered
the great hall, where nobody would
speak one word to him, bad or good.
They went on through the house and found
an orchard on the castle ground.   5110
They had not spoken of their need
for stables, but the men believed
the horses were already theirs
and stabled them well, so who cares?

I think they were too confident.
The owners' health is excellent.
The horses, though, had oats and hay
and litter to their ribs that day.

So at this time the lord Yvain
5120   went in the orchard with his train.
A rich man lay there at his ease
on a silk cloth beneath the trees.
His hand and elbow propped his head.
Before him was a maid who read
a long romance. (I don't know who
composed the tale.) A lady, too,
came in the orchard, and she lay
upon the cloth to listen. They
were the maid's parents, and indeed,
5130   they liked to see and hear her read,
because they had no other child.
She was a well-bred maiden, mild
and beautiful, not yet sixteen.
The God of Love, if he had seen
the maiden, would have made a vow
to serve her. He would not allow
the gentle maid to love or choose
another man. He would refuse
divinity just for her sake,
5140   so he could be a man, and take
and strike his body with the dart,
whose wound heals only by the art
of some base doctor who might care
for Love's wound. But it is not fair
for anyone to heal, unless
he should encounter faithlessness,
for otherwise, to be cured of
these wounds means it was not true love.

[152]

Now, if the story pleased you well,
there's much about these wounds I'd tell,   5150
until I'd finished. I expect
to find that someone would object
and say that I had told you of
my dreams, for people do not love
or fall in love the way they did,
so they are anxious to forbid
a word about it! I will say
instead the manner and the way
the lord Yvain was lodged and kept.
The people in the orchard leapt   5160
upon their feet the moment they
saw him come in and said, "This way,
my lord, may all you have and you
be blessed with all that God can do!"

I do not know if they deceived him,
but everybody there received him
with joy and took great care to feign
how much they hoped the lord Yvain
would be pleased with his bed and board.
The only daughter of the lord   5170
attended him and did her best
to honor such a worthy guest.
The maid removed his armor and
she washed his neck and face and hands.
Her father said that she must wait
upon their guest in fitting state,
so she did everything she might.
Out of her closet she took white
pants and a shirt and sleeves. She sped
to find a needle and some thread,   5180
and sewed them on and clothed him. May
God grant that he won't have to pay

[153]

too much for such attentive hovering!
She gave him a new surcoat, covering
the shirt, and an untorn cloak to wear
around his neck, of silk-dyed vair.
She served him so well, he became
embarrassed and was filled with shame.
The maiden, though, was so well bred,
5190 sincere, and gracious, that instead
it seemed to her she couldn't do
enough for Sir Yvain. She knew
her mother would insist that she
do everything for him, so he
would not be able to complain.
That night at supper, Sir Yvain
was served with many dishes, such
a number, it was far too much.
Then men who brought the dishes might
5200 well have been very tired. That night
he went to bed with even more
respect; no one went near his door
to trouble him. The lion lay
at his feet in his usual way.
At dawn, when God lit His great light
for the world, as early as was right
for one who did as form decreed,
the lord Yvain arose with speed.
He and his maid began to search
5210 until they found the castle church.
They heard Mass, said with uttermost
speed, honoring the Holy Ghost.

The lord Yvain, when the Mass ended,
heard evil news when he intended
to leave. He thought that he was free
to go, but found it could not be

[154]

as he desired. "If you'll allow,"
he said, "sir, I will leave you now."
"My friend, I cannot give you leave,"
the lord replied, "for I must cleave   5220
to a rule dreadful and compelling
which we observe within this dwelling,
and which I must maintain. I shall
send two of my men in the hall,
and both of them are huge and strong.
Against these two men, right or wrong,
you must bear arms and fight. If you
can overcome and kill the two,
my daughter wants you as her spouse,
and everything inside this house   5230
and outside it, sir, you will gain."
"I don't want them," said Sir Yvain.
"May God give me no revenue,
and may your daughter stay with you.
The emperor of Germany
would gladly wed the girl, for she
is beautiful and dignified."
"Be still, fair guest," the lord replied.
"It is quite useless to decline;
you can't escape from our design.   5240
The same man who can overcome
the two men, who are going to come
to test their strength with you in battle,
receives in turn my land, my castle,
and weds my daughter; it's his right.
There's no way to refuse the fight.
The custom here is old and strong
and will continue all too long.
My daughter never will be wed
until I see them crushed or dead."   5250
"I see that I shall have to fight

[155]

against my will," replied the knight.
"I'd pass it by most willingly,
I promise you! But I'll agree
to fight your two men in the fray,
because there is no better way."

The devil's sons came to attack,
and they were hideous and black.
Each held a club, hard, strong, and good,
5260 with hornlike spikes, of cornel wood,
well covered with a copper plate,
and wound with brass for greater weight.
The fiends wore armor to the knee,
but left their heads and faces free,
and their legs too, which were not thin.
Thus armed, the devil's sons came in
and held before their faces light,
strong, round shields, ready for the fight.
The lion started trembling when
5270 he saw them, for he knew the men
came with the weapons that they brought
to strike his master as they fought.
The lion shook with rage. He'd dare
to fight with them! He raised his hair
and thrashed the hard ground with his tail,
for he was planning to assail
the fiends and save the lord Yvain,
before the demons had him slain.
But when they saw the lion, they
5280 said, "Vassal, take this lion away,
for he is threatening us, sir, and
you'll yield or do as we command,
and take your lion out of here,
so that he cannot interfere
to help you or to do us harm.

[156]

You must enjoy our sport of arms
alone! We see the lion would
be glad to help you, if he could."
"If you are so concerned about
the lion, you may take him out   5290
yourselves," the lord Yvain replied,
"for I'd be pleased and satisfied,
if he could do some harm to you,
and I would be delighted to
have help from him!" "Oh, no, you shall
obtain no help from him at all!"
they told him, "Do the best you can,
you'll have no help from any man;
you'll fight alone against us two.
For if the lion were with you   5300
and could attack us on his own,
we would not fight with you alone,
but two against two. So obey
the rules and take your lion away,
whether you like it, sir, or not."
"Where shall I put him, then? What spot
would suit you? Where shall he remain
while we fight?" asked the lord Yvain.
They found a small room and replied,
"Go shut the lion up inside."   5310
"Just as you wish," he said, and he
locked up the lion with the key.

The other people present sought
for armor to protect him, brought
the lord Yvain's horse from its stall,
so he could ride it in the hall.
The champions rushed at him. They meant
to hurt him and felt confident;
the lion had been shut inside

5320 the room. With their clubs they applied
such hard blows that he found his shield
and helmet failed him on the field.
The helmet shattered in a trice,
and then the shield dissolved like ice.
They made holes in the shield that you
could put your fist completely through.
The demons' blows were dreadful ones.
What did he do to the fiend's sons?
The lord, spurred on by shame and fright,

5330 fought for his life with all his might.
He stretched and strained each nerve and chose
to strike back hard and heavy blows.
The devil's sons could only gain
by their gifts, for the lord Yvain
returned the devils' kindness doubled.
The lion's heart was sad and troubled.
Within the room he had begun
to think how Sir Yvain had done
a noble and a kindly deed

5340 for him, and knew that he must need
assistance and the lion's aid.
The lion, if he could evade
his captors, would pay his account;
he'd measure out the full amount
of Sir Yvain's kind deed without
discounting it. He looked about
but could not think of any way.
He heard the blows fall in the fray
and knew it was a wicked fight.

5350 The lion roared with all his might
in rage, and nearly went insane,
and was beside himself with pain.
Next to the door, he looked around
and found it rotten near the ground.

Immediately the lion clawed
the threshold, and he squeezed and pawed,
until he'd struggled through the door
up to his haunches and no more.
The lion saw the lord Yvain
hard pressed, and sweating, and in pain, 5360
because he found the giants great,
and strong, and vile, and obstinate.
He'd felt hard blows from their attack;
as best he could, he'd paid them back,
but had not hurt the demons, since
the two of them knew how to fence
too well, and the light shields they bore
could not be harmed by any sword,
however tempered, and well made,
and strong, and sharp might be the blade. 5370
And so the lord Yvain was right
to fear his own death in the fight,
but he had held his own before
the moment when, beneath the door,
the lion crawled out. So I vow
that if the demons aren't killed now,
they never will be. It's no use
to ask the lion for a truce,
as long as he sees either one
alive! He pulled one devil's son 5380
down like a tree trunk to the ground.
The demons quailed. You would have found
no person there who did not start
rejoicing deep within his heart.
The demon whom the lion struck
won't get up without help or luck!
But then the other demon ran
to help him out, which was a plan
to keep himself safe, lest the lion

5390 first kill his brother, and then fly on
him afterward. He's more afraid
of the lion than his master's blade!
The lord Yvain would have been mad,
when he could see the demon had
his back to him, quite unaware
he'd left his neck exposed and bare,
if he had spared his life when he
had such an opportunity!
So, when the rascal had disclosed
5400 his head and neck, bare and exposed,
the lord Yvain struck such a blow,
he cut the demon's head off so
fast that he never knew a word
about it. Sir Yvain preferred
to spare the fiend the lion held
down on the floor, completely quelled,
so he dismounted, but in vain.
The fiend had suffered so much pain,
no doctor would have time to save
5410 the demon's life. The lion gave
such a bad wound in rage and hate,
that he'd been in a dreadful state
since the time of the first attack.
The knight did drag the lion back
to help save him, in any case,
and saw his shoulder torn from place.
He did not fear the devil's might;
the devil lay there, still, and white,
and helpless, like a dead man, and
5420 his club had fallen from his hand.
Although the fiend was very weak,
somehow he found the strength to speak.
He pleaded, "Fair sir, take away
your lion, please, so that he may

do me no more harm. You may do
with me whatever pleases you.
But anyone who has despaired
and begged for mercy should be spared,
unless he's found a cruel man.
I won't fight any more; I can   5430
not rise without your help or stand.
I put myself within your hands."
He answered, "Speak then, and concede
that you are vanquished." "Sir, indeed,"
the devil's son said to the knight,
"it's clear I'm overcome, in spite
of all my efforts. I'll concede
the fight, I swear it." "Then you need
not fear me or my lion," said
the lord Yvain. The people sped   5440
to him and formed a group in haste.

The lord and lady both embraced
the knight with joy, and to reward
the lord Yvain, said, "You'll be lord
and master of us, and our daughter
will be your lady, for we've brought her
to give you as a wife." "And I
shall give her back," was his reply.
"I don't care; he who wants her may
have her, although I do not say   5450
this from contempt. Don't be upset,
for I'm unable to accept
your daughter, though you want to give her.
But rather, if you please, deliver
the wretched maidens to my care.
As both of you are well aware,
before the battle we agreed
that all the maidens would be freed."

The lord said, "What you say is true,
5460 and I deliver them to you
quite freely. But you've also known
that you must take all that I own
and wed my daughter. She is wise,
and rich, and lovely: realize
you'll never find a fairer wife
or richer marriage in your life."
"My lord, you do not understand
my business and my duties, and
I am not going to explain
5470 them to you," said the lord Yvain.
"I have refused what no man would
refuse if he were free and could
devote all of his heart and mind
to a fair, noble maid. You'd find
that if I could, I'd gladly take her,
but I cannot accept or make her
or anyone my wife. Please know
that this is true, and let me go.
The maid who kept me company
5480 and came here with me waits for me,
and I shall not abandon her,
whatever happens." "What, fair sir?
You want to go away? But how?
You'll never leave till I allow,
until I change my mind and state
that they may open up the gate!
You will remain here in my strong
fast prison; you are proud and wrong,
when I have asked you, sir, to choose
5490 to wed my daughter, to refuse!"
"Upon my word, I don't disdain
your daughter, but I can't remain
and marry her! No, I must ride

on with the maid who is my guide.
I have no choice. If you command,
sir, I will pledge with my right hand,
so you'll believe me, and I'll vow
that, just as you see me here now,
I will return, if I can, and
I will accept your daughter's hand."   5500
"Confound it, who asked you to swear
you would return? For if you care
about my daughter, and you find
she's noble, beautiful, and kind,
you'll soon be back! But you could take
no oath or promise that would make
you come back sooner. Go on, now;
you're free from every oath and vow.
Moreover, sir, if storms detain
your coming, or high winds and rain,   5510
or nothing, sir, I do not care,
because I do not hold my fair
young daughter so cheap as to force
the girl upon you! Mount your horse,
go on, attend to your affair,
for I assure you I don't care
if you go on or if you stay."

The lord Yvain just turned away
and left the castle with some speed.
He led the wretched maidens freed   5520
from prison, whom the rich lord had
delivered to him, poorly clad;
however they felt well-to-do
and left the castle two by two.
They walked before the lord Yvain
and could not feel such joy again,
were He who made the whole world round

to come from Heaven to the ground.
To join the maids, the people came,
5530   who'd said as much to cause him shame
as they could ever find to say.
They walked with him part of the way
and asked peace and forgiveness, and
he said he didn't understand.
"What's this you're saying?" said the knight,
"I haven't harbored any spite
against you, for as I recall,
you did not slander me at all."
The people liked the things that he
5540   had said and praised his courtesy.
They went with him for a long space,
commending him to Heaven's grace.
The maidens, after taking leave,
went on their way, and I believe
that when they left, they made a bow
and prayed the Lord God would allow
the lord Yvain to end his quest,
and grant him great joy and the best
of health wherever he might go.
5550   He answered, "May God save you," so
concerned was he with the delay.
"Go to your lands," he told them. "May
God grant you health and happiness."
They went their way with joyfulness.

RETURN TO KING ARTHUR'S COURT

HE took another road and pressed
so hard he did not stop to rest
one day that week. The demoiselle

[164]

knew the road back extremely well
and led him to the place she'd left
the disinherited, bereft,   5560
poor, younger sister. When she learned
the news the maiden had returned
and brought the Knight with the Lion, there
was never joy that could compare
with the great joy within her heart.
She thought her sister'd grant a part
of her inheritance if she
insisted. Until recently
the maid had been so ill, she'd lain
in bed. She'd managed to regain   5570
her health, but still her malady
affected her strength seriously;
her features made it evident.
The maiden ran out first and went
to welcome them without delay.
She honored them in every way.
No need to tell of the delight
there was inside the house that night!
No mention will be made of it;
it takes too long, so I omit   5580
all that occurred until next day
when they arose and went their way.
They rode on, and kept traveling,
and reached the castle where the king
had stayed for fourteen days or more.
The elder sister was there, for
she'd kept close to court and arrived
to await the sister she'd deprived.
Although the time was drawing near,
she did not worry much or fear.   5590
She doubted that her sister would
find any warrior who could

[165]

withstand the lord Gawain's attacking.
Of those two weeks, one day was lacking.
Now if this day had passed, the fight
in truth, by judgment and by right,
would have been settled so she'd win.
She does not know what's standing in
her way! Because the lord Yvain
5600   and maid decided to remain
where nobody knew them at all,
they lodged outside the castle wall
in a hut. If they'd stayed inside,
they knew they would be recognized
by everybody, and that they
did not desire. At break of day
they left but hid as best they might
until the sun was strong and bright.
I don't know how to ascertain
5610   how many days the lord Gawain
had been away, so nobody
at court knew of him except she
for whom he would be fighting, for
he went in hiding three or four
leagues off and came back in disguise.
No one at court could recognize
him, even people who, before,
had known him by the arms he bore.
The maid, who clearly meant to claim
5620   her sister's share of the land, came
to court quite early to present
the lord Gawain, because she meant
to use his help to win the fight
in which she hadn't any right.
The maid came to King Arthur. "Sire,
my sister's two weeks soon expire.
The noon hour's almost passed away,

and this day is the final day.
Now you can see how much I care
about defending my fair share.   5630
Perhaps it would make sense to wait,
if we thought she'd arrive this late,
but I may praise the Lord that she
will not return, for obviously
she can do nothing to regain
her land, and she has tried in vain.
I have been ready to defend
my land until the very end
of this day. It is mine by right,
but I have won without a fight.   5640
So I will leave your court now, and
go unopposed to claim my land,
and to my sister I will give
no part as long as I shall live,
and she will live in misery
and wretchedness." The king could see
the maid was wrong; her only care
was to be hateful and unfair
to her young sister. At the end
he said, "In royal courts, my friend,   5650
while the king's seated, you must wait
as long as I deliberate.
No cheating! It's too soon to pack;
I think your sister will come back
in time." And then the king caught sight,
while he was speaking, of the Knight
with the Lion, and the maiden too.
They came alone, because the two
had slipped out of the hut that day
and left the lion behind, to stay   5660
where they had spent the night. The king
had seen the maiden entering

his court; he made his pleasure plain
at having seen the girl again.
King Arthur took the destitute
young sister's side in the dispute,
because the king knew wrong from right.
The king cried out in his delight,
"God save you, lovely one, come here!"

5670 The elder sister, too, could hear
King Arthur's greeting, and she shook.
She turned around to take a look
and saw her sister and the knight
she'd brought back to defend her right;
her face turned blacker than the ground.
The courtiers welcomed the maid, who found
the king and went where he was seated.
She stood before him, and she greeted
the king: "God save the king," said she,

5680 "and all his court and family.
If, in this quarrel, King, my right
may be defended by a knight,
here is one now, whom I must thank
for following me here. This frank
and noble knight had much to do
but felt so sorry for me, too,
that he resolved to put aside
his projects to defend my side.
My lady sister, who is dear

5690 to me, and whom I both revere
and love like my own heart, Sire, would
be courteous and very good
to give me back my rightful share.
To do so would be only fair;
I'm asking for no land of hers."
"I'm asking for no land of yours!
You have no land and never will!"

[168]

she answered. "You could talk until
you dried up with your sorrow, and
your words won't get you any land!"   5700

The younger sister, who was wise
and courteous, made polite replies.
"To see two men of such repute
do battle for our small dispute
is hard for me, but all the same
I cannot set aside my claim;
I need my portion of the land."
"Whoever answered your demand
would be a fool," her sister boasted.
"May I go up in flames, be toasted   5710
in hellfire, if I ever give
a bit of land to you to live
upon in comfort! No, the Seine
and Danube will have joined banks, when
I've chosen to decline this fight!"
"Then may the Lord God and my right,
in which I've placed great trust alway,
protect and aid the knight today,
who, out of love and righteousness,
has come to serve me and redress   5720
my wrongs, although we do not know
each other very well." And so
they talked while there were things to say,
and then they led their knights away
out to the courtyard. Everyone
went out too, as is always done,
to see blows fall in battles, fights,
and fencing matches. But the knights,
who are going to fight, don't recognize
each other, though throughout their lives   5730
they've loved each other like a brother!

[169]

DO they no longer love each other?
Yes, I would answer you, and no;
and I will prove that this is so.
Each answer's right. The lord Gawain
sincerely loves the lord Yvain,
fights by his side in war and game;
and Sir Yvain has done the same
for Sir Gawain, when there was need.
If Sir Yvain had realized, he'd
have greeted Sir Gawain instead;
he would be glad to give his head
for him before he'd strike one blow.
His friend would do the same, I know.
Is that not perfect Love and true?
Of course! But Hate is present too,
and so you must make no mistake,
because the knights intend to break
each other's heads, and do great damage
and all the harm that they can manage.

I wonder how a Love so great
can coexist with mortal Hate?
How can two things so opposite
be lodged in the same house? For it
appears to me that they could not
be found together in one spot,
or even spend a single night
without a quarrel or a fight,
as soon as Love or Hate could sense
the other one in residence.
Still, in a building, there may be
many a hall and balcony

[170]

and bedroom found throughout the place.
I think that this must be the case.
Love's in one of the hidden nooks;
Hate's on the balcony, and looks
out on the road, and wants to try
to be seen by all passers-by.
Hate's in the saddle and will spur
5770   ahead of Love, who cannot stir.
Oh, Love, what has become of you?
Come, see what they're about to do!
Look at the armies of your foes,
and learn the men who strike the blows
are the same men we're speaking of,
who love with such a sacred love.
A Love which is not feigned or vile
is rare and holy. All this while
Love has been blind, and Hate can't see,
5780   for if Love saw these two men, she
would have forbidden either knight
to harm his friend or start to fight.
So Love is blind, filled with dismay,
confused, beguiled, and led astray.
She's seen these men, but hasn't known
she ought to claim them as her own,
and even though Hate cannot say
why the two knights should fight that day
or hate each other; as we've stated,
5790   he fills them full of mortal hatred.

No man will love the man who's aimed
to kill or make him feel ashamed.
What? Does the lord Yvain intend
to kill the lord Gawain, his friend?
Yes; Sir Gawain has planned to kill
the lord Yvain, of his free will.

[171]

But would the lord Gawain have planned
to kill his friend with his own hand,
or to do worse than I have said?
5800   I swear that he would not. Instead,
by all that God has done for man,
I swear the knights would never plan
to harm each other, for the land
the Roman Empire could command.
But I have told some ugly lies,
for everyone must realize
how much each warrior wants to vie
with his foe, with his lance raised high
in rest position; each will maim
5810   the other knight, and cause him shame,
and seek to do him injury,
make no mistake!
                  Now answer me:
suppose one warrior overcame
the other: can the loser blame
his friend for striking such a blow?
For if they come to blows, I know
the knights won't say the fight is done
until it's clear which side has won.
Would Sir Yvain be right to say,
5820   if he's defeated in the fray,
the man who caused him harm and shame
has never called him any name
but "friend" and "comrade" and intends
to number him among his friends
forever? If, by fortune's whim,
the lord Yvain should injure him
or win the fight, would Sir Gawain
have any reason to complain?
No, he will not know whom to blame;
5830   they do not know each other's name.

THE knights drew back, turned to advance,
and when they met and struck, each lance,
though thick and made of strong ash, broke.
But neither of the two knights spoke
a single word; in that event,
the outcome would be different.
No blow would be struck in that case;
they would come running to embrace
and kiss each other, rather than
attack each other. But each man   5840
began to strike and wound his friend.
Their swords and shields began to bend;
their helmets filled with dents and split,
their swordblades were the worse for it:
they nicked and dulled the blades; struck at
each other with the edge, not the flat
part of the blade; and gave such blows
with the sword pommels on the nose-
guards and the cheeks and brows and necks,
both knights turned black and blue where flecks   5850
of blood formed underneath the skin.
Their hauberks tore, their shields broke in
small pieces. Neither knight that day
escaped unhurt, so hard did they
exert themselves; to such extent
that each knight's breath was almost spent.
The jacinths and the emeralds set
to decorate each fighter's helmet
became demolished on the spot,
because the battle was so hot.   5860
They struck on helmets, and they used
their pommels till they were confused.

The lord Yvain and Sir Gawain
almost beat out each other's brain.
Their eyes in their heads gleamed and shone,
as with strong nerves, and good, hard bone,
and clenched fists, great and square and stout,
they struck each other on the snout
as long as they could hold their swords,
5870 which were most useful when the lords
wished to strike hard. Both men were strong,
and since they were, the fight was long.
But when the knights had struck and hacked,
until their shields were bent and cracked,
and each had crushed the other's crest,
both knights drew back a bit to rest.
Their veins were pounding; their breath fled.
The knights did not rest long; instead
they fought more fiercely than before
5880 and hurt each other even more.
Then everybody said that they
had seen no knights before that day
with greater courage. "No, this test
is no game. They have done their best,
and they will never have, in turn,
the honors that their merits earn."

The two friends fighting overheard
and knew that people now preferred
to reconcile the sisters; they
5890 were trying hard to find a way.
The elder sister'd not consent
to any sort of settlement.
The younger sister said that she
would trust the king's ability
to judge and would accept her fate.
The elder was so obstinate;

[174]

Queen Guinevere, the men who knew
the laws well, knights, King Arthur too;
all took the younger sister's side.
They asked King Arthur to decide.   5900
They thought a third or quarter share
to the young sister would be fair.
He should ignore the elder's rights
and separate the warring knights
who'd shown such courage and such fame,
for it would be a dreadful shame
if one knight hurt the other one, or
deprived his enemy of honor.
The king said he would not consent
to take part in a settlement   5910
to which the elder would not agree,
since she behaved so wickedly.
His words were overheard by those
knights who were landing such hard blows,
that they astonished everyone.
The battle had not yet been won.
In fact, the valiant knights were tied,
and no one watching could decide
who was the better knight. They bought
renown with anguish as they fought.   5920
Both were amazed and both despaired
that they were so exactly paired.
Each warrior wondered who could stand
his onslaught with such courage, and
so long did the two warriors fight,
that day was turning into night.
Their arms were tired, their bodies lame,
their blood was boiling hot, and came
bubbling forth from many places
upon the warriors' frames and faces,   5930
and flowed and trickled down from under

their hauberks. So it is no wonder
the two knights, who were so hard pressed,
were wishing they could take some rest.

And so the warring knights withdrew
to rest again, and each knight knew,
despite his triumphs in the past,
that he had met his match at last.
For a long time they did not dare
5940   take up their arms. They rested there,
and neither warrior wished to fight,
since day was darkening to night,
and furthermore, the way they'd fought
made them respect each other. The thought
kept them apart, and made them cease
to fight, and urged them to make peace.
Before the two knights leave the field,
their real names will have been revealed,
and there'll be peace and joy again
5950   between the two. The lord Yvain
spoke first, because he was polite
and brave. But when he spoke, the knight
who was his good friend, did not know
who he was, for his voice was low,
and weak, and broken, very hoarse,
because his blood was stirred, of course,
by all the blows he'd undergone.
"My lord," he said, "night's coming on,
and I don't think we'll be to blame
5960   if night parts us. But I can claim
that I admire you greatly, for
at no time in my life before
did I fight in, or undertake,
a battle which has made me ache

[176]

as terribly as did our fight.
I've never heard of any knight
whom I would be so pleased to meet,
because I thought I'd taste defeat.
So I admire you greatly, and
I say that you know how to land   5970
your blows well, and how to make good
use of them. I'd not thought I would
receive such dreadful blows from any
knight! I've never felt as many
hard blows as you have given me,
and those head blows, especially!"
"My word," replied the lord Gawain,
"you're not so stunned or in such pain
but that I'm not as much or more.
The simple truth would please you, for   5980
if I lent anything at all,
you've paid me, interest, principal,
the whole sum! You gave, I believe,
more gladly than I did receive!
But, sir, however that may be,
you want to know what men call me,
so I won't hide it. I'm Gawain,
King Lot's son." When the lord Yvain
had heard this news, then he became
amazed and troubled at the name.   5990
Grief stricken and enraged, the lord
Yvain threw down his bloody sword
and broken shield, and after he'd
dismounted, stood beside his steed
and cried, "Oh, no! What awful luck!
What ignorance! Because we struck
each other fighting in disguise,
and so we did not recognize

each other! If I'd realized who
6000 you were, I'd not have fought with you;
I'd not have struck one single blow!
I would have given up, I know!"
"What's this?" replied the lord Gawain.
"Now who are you?" "I am Yvain,
who loves you more than anyone
the wide world round, beneath the sun,
and you have always loved me, and
you've honored me throughout the land
in every court. Now I want to
6010 repent, and make amends to you,
and do you honor. I'll declare
I'm overcome in this affair."
"Sir, would you do so much for me?"
said noble lord Gawain. "I'd be
presumptuous and insolent,
if I took such a settlement.
The honor's yours, for I resign.
The victory never will be mine!"
"Oh, fair sir, do not say that, for
6020 I know I can't stand any more,
I am so hurt and so fatigued!"
His friend and comrade said, "You need
not be concerned, companion,
for I'm defeated and undone,
and I don't say it to be kind.
Throughout the world, you couldn't find
a man to whom I'd not say those
words rather than receive more blows."

The lord Gawain dismounted too,
6030 and left his horse, and each knight threw
his arms around the other. They

[178]

embraced, and they went on to say
each one had lost. Their arguing
was still in progress when the king
and barons ran up at the sight
of peace and truce to end the fight.
Because he greatly wished to know
the names of those men who were so
delighted and agreed so well,
the king addressed them. "My lords, tell   6040
the way this sudden harmony
and friendship ever came to be,
when we have seen you both display
such hatred on the field today?"
King Arthur's nephew, Sir Gawain,
said, "Sire, we're going to explain
the dreadful stroke of luck that brought
about the battle we have fought.
Because you've come and waited here
to learn what happened, you should hear   6050
the truth. Your nephew, I, Gawain,
did not know he was Sir Yvain,
my comrade and my friend, till he
had asked my name first, luckily.
God willed it so. When each one came
and told the other one his name,
we knew each other; not before
each of us had been waging war
against the other for some time.
If we'd fought any longer, I'm   6060
sure I'd have weakened. By my head,
I'm certain that I would be dead,
because of his strength, and because
the elder sister's evil cause
had put me on the battlefield.

So now, I would prefer to yield
to him; that's better, I contend,
than dying fighting with a friend!"

The lord Yvain felt his blood stir.
6070 "So help me God, my dear, fair sir,"
he said, "you have no right to tell
my lord the king that; you know well
that in this fight *I* was the one
who was defeated and undone!"
"No, I was!" "No, I was!" And so
each valiant lord wished to bestow
the crown of victory in the fight
on his best friend, because each knight
was far too noble to accept
6080 the honor for himself and kept
attempting to tell everyone
the other warrior had won.
King Arthur chose to end the fight
when he had listened to each knight
a while. King Arthur liked to see
two knights who'd done great injury,
who were hurt badly, everyplace,
and who were willing to embrace.
"My lords," the king said, "it's clear, then,
6090 there is great love between you when
each one surrenders! In exchange,
I do believe I can arrange
the matter, if you want me to,
so everyone will honor you
as valiant men and praise me." They
both promised that they would obey
and do all that he specified.
The king announced he would decide

the quarrel righteously and well.
"Where is the wicked demoiselle,   6100
who took her sister's portion and
insisted that she leave the land,
and was so cruel to her?" said he.
"I'm here, Sire," she said instantly.
"What, are you there? Come over here.
I thought that it was very clear
that you had disinherited
your younger sister. Since you've said
the truth to me, I now declare
you must resign her rightful share.   6110
Henceforth her rights won't be denied."
"Oh, my lord king! If I replied
so thoughtlessly, it's so absurd.
You shouldn't take me at my word!
For Heaven's sake, Sire, don't reject me!
You are the king and must protect me
against wrongdoing and mistrial!"
King Arthur answered, "That's why I'll
return your sister's rightful share.
I've never wished to be unfair,   6120
and you have clearly heard them tell
the way your knight, and hers as well,
agreed upon complete concession
of the dispute to my discretion.
You're going to hate my words and tone,
for your wrongdoing is well known.
Each knight declares he lost the fight,
in honor of the other knight,
so there's no reason to delay.
You'll do exactly as I say,   6130
without resisting, utterly,
since the dispute's been left to me;

[181]

or, if you say that you've been cheated,
I'll say my nephew was defeated.
That is the worst thing for your part,
and it would go against my heart."

He'd not have done it, but he meant
to frighten her, so she'd consent
to give her sister, out of fright,
6140   the land to which she had a right,
because it was so very clear:
unless induced by force or fear,
the elder wouldn't yield a thing,
despite the urging of the king.
In fear and dread they heard her say,
"Now I can see I must obey;
I have to yield to your desire,
although my heart is grieving, Sire.
It's very difficult for me,
6150   but she'll have what is rightfully
her part of my land; I pledge your
own body, Sire, so she'll be sure."

"Endow her with the land outright,"
the king said, "so she'll be by right
your vassal woman, holding land
from you. Love her as vassal, and
she will love you, as you assist her,
as her liege lady and her sister."
The king conducted the affair,
6160   until the maiden claimed her share
of land and thanked King Arthur too.
King Arthur asked his nephew, who
was a brave, valiant knight, if he
would please permit himself to be

[182]

disarmed, and asked the lord Yvain
to do the same as Sir Gawain
and let them take his arms. By now
they did not need them anyhow.
The two knights laid their arms aside
and kissed. The court agreed they'd tied.   6170
But while the two knights were embracing,
both of them saw the lion racing
in their direction, for he sought
the lord Yvain, and when he caught
sight of his master, he expressed
his joyfulness, and then the best
men drew away, and you well might
have seen the boldest take to flight.

The lord Yvain said, "Everyone
stand still! Why do you want to run,   6180
since nobody is chasing you?
Don't be afraid the lion will do
you any harm—believe me! He
is mine and I am his, and we
are both comrades-in-arms." And then
the truth was clear to all the men
who'd heard of the adventures told
about the knight and lion bold:
the lord Yvain was the defiant
knight who had killed the wicked giant!   6190
"Sir comrade," Sir Gawain exclaimed,
"God help me, I am so ashamed!
To think how poorly I've repaid
your services to me and aid!
You killed the giant to release
my nephews and to save my niece!
I've thought about you without pause

[183]

and could not calm myself, because
I'd heard of no knight I could say
6200 that I had known, until today,
in any land I'd set my eye on,
whom people called 'the Knight with the Lion.' "

By then they'd laid their arms aside.
The lion ran up with long strides
to the place where his master sat
and showed all joy and gladness that
a dumb beast can show. They attest
both knights were led away to rest
in sickrooms: after that disaster,
6210 they needed doctors and some plaster
to treat their wounds. King Arthur, who
loved both knights dearly, had the two
brought to his bedroom and sent for
a good physician, who knew more
of surgery than any man.
He strove to cure them, and began
to treat their wounds as best he might.

THE RECONCILIATION

BUT when the doctor'd cured each knight,
the lord Yvain, whose heart was set
6220 on love, saw he could not forget
or go on living out his life.
He'd die of love unless his wife
took pity on him. They aver
he nearly died of love for her.
So he decided he would start

from Arthur's court alone, depart,
and go and wage war at the spring,
and he would cause such thundering,
such lightning, and such sheets of rain,
that by necessity again,   6230
he'd force the lady to make peace,
or otherwise, he'd never cease
to rile her fountain and cause rain
and high winds. So the lord Yvain
left court, and no one knew or heard
more of him, when his wounds were cured.
He had his lion by his side,
who stayed with him until he died,
and never left the knight again.
The lion and the lord Yvain   6240
went on until they saw the spring.
They made it rain. The thundering
and lightning were so violent,
that nobody could tell one-tenth
of it, because it seemed as though
the forest would fall down and go
in Hell's abyss! So it appeared
to those in town! The lady feared
her castle would collapse that day;
she saw the walls and tower sway.   6250
The bravest man would much prefer
to be a Turkish prisoner
in Persia than be near that wall.
The people were so scared, they all
swore at their ancestors, long dead.
"Damn the first man," the people said,
"who chose to build this castle and
construct a house upon this land,
for in the whole world, he could not

[185]

6260 discover a more hateful spot!
One man is able to invade,
torment, and make us all afraid!"

"Now, in this matter you must get
advice, my lady," said Lunette,
"and you will find no one, indeed,
to help you in this time of need,
unless you seek him far off, for
within this castle, nevermore
will we feel safe or dare to go
6270 beyond the walls and gate. You know
if you had someone here you might
ask to assemble every knight
in your domain, for this affair
your finest knights would never dare
step forward. If you must surrender
to storms because you've no defender
to guard your fountain, you'll appear
ridiculous, shamed, filled with fear.
Won't you be honored when they've learned
6280 that your attacker has returned
to his domain without a fight!
You will be in a sorry plight,
if you can't think of some way to
resolve the situation." "You,"
replied the lady, "who are wise,
tell me what plan I can devise,
and I will follow your advice."
"My lady, if I knew a nice
plan, I would offer it, indeed.
6290 But now you are in greatest need
of a much wiser counselor.
I won't intrude; I will endure,
with all the rest, the wind and rain

[186]

until, please God, I see again
some brave man in your court, who might
accept the burden of this fight.
My lady, I am forced to say
I doubt he will appear today,
and I am sure the worst is yet
to come!" The lady told Lunette,   6300
"Say something else, mademoiselle!
Within my town no people dwell
whom I could ask to do one thing
to guard the great stone and the spring.
But now, please God, let us hear your
advice and your opinion, for
they always say that one can test
one's friends in time of need the best."

"My lady, if we knew the land
where he who conquered three knights and   6310
the giant lives, we would be wise
to search for him; but I surmise
as long as that brave knight believes
his lady hates him, while he grieves,
no man or woman will persuade
the knight to come and give him aid,
unless that person shows that he
will use all his ability
to make his lady hate him less.
He's dying of unhappiness."   6320
The lady said, "I'm ready now
to pledge my word to you and vow,
before you look for him, that I'll
do all I can to reconcile
the knight and lady, but persuade
the knight to come and bring me aid!"
Lunette said, "Lady, I've no doubt

that you will quickly bring about
a truce and end the discontent
6330   between the two, if you consent.
If you have no objections, though,
I'll take your oath before I go."
The lady answered, "I don't mind."

Polite Lunette asked them to find
a precious relic, which they brought her.
The lady knelt. So Lunette caught her
by playing Truth! Administering
the oath, she overlooked no thing
that might be advantageous and
6340   good to insert. "Now raise your hand!
Tomorrow I won't have you lay
the blame on me in any way.
What you do is no help to me;
it's for your own prosperity!
Please swear that you will do your best
in the Knight with the Lion's interest,
until he knows that by your art
he will possess his lady's heart
as wholly as he did before."
6350   The lady raised her hand and swore:
"So help me God and saints, as you
have said to me, so I say too.
My heart will never fail, and I
will do all I can do, and try,
if I have the ability,
to help restore the love that he
knew that his lady felt before."

Lunette had done her work well, for
there was no thing that she desired
6360   as much as that which had transpired.

[188]

A palfrey with an easy pace
was brought out. With a cheerful face
and mind she rode till she had seen
the knight beside the evergreen;
the one she had not thought she'd find
so near by. She'd made up her mind
to search for him throughout the land,
before she found him close at hand.
Lunette had recognized the knight
by the lion. When she had caught sight   6370
of him, she sped toward the renowned
knight and dismounted to hard ground.
The lord Yvain had seen Lunette
far off, and recognized, and met,
and greeted her as she alighted.
She said, "My lord, I'm so delighted
that I've discovered you nearby!"
The lord Yvain said in reply,
"Why? Were you looking for me?" "Yes!
I haven't felt such happiness   6380
since I was born! My lady swore
an oath that she would be once more
your lady; you her lord as well.
This is the truth, sir, that I tell,
provided she won't break her word."

The splendid news that he had heard
brought great joy to the lord Yvain;
he'd not thought he'd hear that again!
With joy he started to embrace
Lunette and kiss her eyes and face,   6390
since she had managed to obtain
his happiness. The lord Yvain
said, "Truly, I cannot repay
this deed, sweet friend, in any way.

I am afraid I won't have strength
and time enough throughout the length
of my life to repay and serve
you as well as you now deserve."
"Sir," she said, "have no fear, and do

6400 not let that thought start troubling you!
You have enough ability
and time for others and for me.
If I've done what I ought to do,
thank me as much as someone who
borrowed from you and paid his debt.
I don't feel I've repaid you yet!"
"My God, you must have paid that score
five hundred thousand times or more!
When you are ready, let us go.

6410 Have you told her who I am?" "No,
upon my word," Lunette exclaimed,
"she does not know how you are named;
she calls you 'the Knight with the Lion' still!"

But as they talked, they rode until
the knight, the lion, and the maid
came to the castle, and they paid
attention to no women or
men there. Instead they came before
the lady, who was pleased to learn

6420 the news about the maid's return
and that she was accompanied
by the lion and the knight, whom she'd
so wished to see and know and meet.
The lord Yvain fell at her feet
completely armed. Lunette stood by
and said, "Raise him up and apply
all of your power, strength, and skill
to give him back that peace, good will,

and pardon, which no one can do
throughout the world, except for you."   6430
The lady asked the knight to stand.
"All the resources I command
are his; I'll do what's possible
to bring him peace and do his will."
"My lady, if it were not true,
I'd not be saying this to you,"
Lunette said, "but the matter's more
in your power than I said before.
I'm going to tell the whole truth now,
and you will see and will allow   6440
you never had and never can
have a friend better than this man.
God, who desired that there should be
unending love and harmony
between you two, has found a way.
He helped me find him here today.
So I can prove that this is true,
I've just one thing to say to you:
forgive him, put your wrath aside,
you are his lady, and abide   6450
in harmony with him again.
This is your husband, Sir Yvain!"

The lady heard these words, and she
began to tremble. "God save me!
You've trapped me neatly, and in spite
of me, you've made me love a knight
who neither loves nor honors me!
What helpful work you've done for me!
What services you did perform!
I'd rather suffer wind and storm   6460
my whole life long. I would prefer
to have done so, and if it were

not such a horrid thing to break
an oath, the lord would never make
peace or be reconciled with me,
for I am sure the memory
would smolder in me and return
the way flames smolder on and burn
in ashes! But I will refrain
6470 from thinking of it all again,
because we must reach an accord
and be at peace again!" The lord
Yvain heard her and understood
his cause was going well; he would
be reconciled with her again.
"One must have mercy," Sir Yvain
replied, "on sinners. I have had
to pay most dear for being mad.
I was mad to outstay the time.
6480 I know I'm guilty and that I'm
bold to have come to you; however,
if you will keep me, I will never
wrong you again." "Yes," she replied,
"I will consent to this, for I'd
be blamed for perjury if I
did not use all my power to try
to work for peace between us two,
and if you please, that's what we'll do."
"Thank you five hundred times! The Lord,
6490 in all my life, could not reward
or grant to me such uttermost
delight, so help me Holy Ghost!"
The lord is reconciled with her.
No matter what his troubles were,
his joy has never been so great.
It's ended well, and I can state
that he is cherished and adored

by his dear lady, and the lord
Yvain adores her, loves her so,
he has forgotten all his woe   6500
in the great joy without an end
that he feels now with his sweet friend.
Lunette is very happy, then,
for she lacked nothing she wished, when
she'd made unending peace again
between the perfect lord Yvain
and his beloved, perfect friend.

At this point Chrétien will end
his romance *The Knight with the Lion*, for
no one has ever told him more,   6510
and you'll hear no more told, besides,
unless somebody adds some lies.

"Li Chevaliers au Lyeon explycit."
Guiot prepared this manuscript.
His house is close by, in the alley
before Our Lady of the Valley.

NOTES

1. "Britain" is the translation of "Bretagne," or what is today Great Britain and the French province of Brittany. Many Britons had migrated to Brittany after the Saxon conquest in the sixth century, and the people of these regions were linked by ties of kinship and shared an oral tradition of Celtic folklore.

3. Carduel is today Carlisle, in Cumberland near the Scottish border, as T. B. W. Reid notes in Chrétien de Troyes, *Yvain (le chevalier au lion)*, critical text of Wendelin Foerster, introduction, notes and glossary by T. B. W. Reid (Manchester: Manchester University Press, 1942), p. 187.

5–6. Julian Harris mentions that a scholar suggested the rhyme "plentycost / Pentecost," in Chrétien de Troyes, *Yvain, ou le chevalier au lion*, translated by André Mary, with an introduction and notes by Julian Harris (New York: Dell, 1963), p. 31.

18. The degeneracy of love in modern times was a favorite theme of medieval poets, as W. Wistar Comfort notes in Chrétien de Troyes, *Arthurian Romances*, translated by W. Wistar Comfort, Everyman's Library, no. 698 (London: J. M. Dent and Sons, 1914), p. 368. See line 5151ff for another example.

35. At this time French audiences welcomed the Breton legends of adventure, love, and marvel as a change from the epics of Charlemagne and his knights, as Roger Sherman Loomis observes in *The Development of Arthurian Romance* (London: Hutchinson, 1963), p. 33.

46. The thirteenth-century Welsh tale of "The Lady of the Fountain" in *The Mabinogion*, translated by Gwyn Jones and Thomas Jones, Everyman's Library (London: J. M. Dent and Sons, 1949), pp. 155–182, which may have a common source with Chrétien de Troyes's *Yvain* in some older work, is very similar to *Yvain*, both in the general incidents and in many specific details: the king's retiring early (l. 46), the painted room studded with gilded nails (ll. 898–899), the scarlet cushion (l. 1803), and the presence of bishops at the wedding (l. 2009).

53. Reid notes that Kay the seneschal is portrayed by Geoffrey of Monmouth and by Wace as a valiant and chivalrous knight, but that Chrétien portrays him as an evil-tempered braggart and a poor fighter (Chrétien de Troyes, *Yvain*, Foerster, p. 188). The minstrels often portrayed the watchful and economical seneschal as a villain (see l. 3472 for another example). Reid notes that in Chrétien's romances Gawain becomes the ideal knight, invincible in battle and perfect in courtesy.

54. Loomis notes in *Development of Arthurian Romance*, p. 59, and in *Arthurian Tradition and Chrétien de Troyes* (New York: Columbia University Press, 1949), p. 269, that Yvain is one of the few knights in Arthurian literature who actually lived. Owain, son of Urien (a historic king of the district of Rheged, in northern England or southern Scotland) fought triumphantly with his father against the Angles who invaded Northumbria in the latter half of the sixth century (Urban T. Holmes places

him at the Battle of Armterid in 573, in *Chrétien de Troyes*, New York, Twayne, 1970, p. 11). Both Owain and his father won such glory in battle that their names and memory were preserved in Welsh folklore. Owain appears in two tales of *The Mabinogion:* "The Dream of Rhonabwy" and "The Lady of the Fountain." Wace mentions Yvain in *Le roman de Brut* (1155), ll. 13189–13200: "To Ewein, son of Urien, who was highly esteemed by the court, King Arthur gave Scotland as an inheritance, and Ewein paid homage to the King for it; he had been Augissel's neph-ew, and so had a lawful claim to the inheritance, for Augissel had neither son nor wife to rule the land before Ewein. Ewein possessed tremendous courage, and he earned very great fame and honor in the conflict and the war which Modred brought about in England," (ed. Ivor Arnold, vol. 2, Paris: Société des Anciens Textes Fran-çais, 1940).

141. At that time people believed that the heart, not the mind, was the center of reasoning, perception, and emotion.

165. A. C. L. Brown says in *Iwain: Study in the Origins of Arthurian Romance* (New York: Haskell House, 1968) that Calogrenant's tale is written in the tradition of Celtic legends, such as the "Voyage of Bran," about voyages to the Other World. The Other World was a land outside the boundaries of mortal time and space, of perpetual youth and feasting, inhabited by women, and frequently reached by a dangerous passage (ibid., pp. 30 and 58).

166. The expression "as lonely as a countryman" refers to the fact that the peasant traveled alone, whereas the knight was always accompanied by others, as Joseph Reason notes in *An Inquiry into the Structural Style and Originality of Chrétien's Yvain* (Studies in Romance Languages and Literatures, no. 57), Washington, D.C.: Catholic University of America Press, 1958, p. 93.

177. Wace describes Brocéliande Forest and the fountain of Berenton in *Le roman de Rou* (1160–1174): "Brocéliande, of which the Bretons frequently tell tales, is a very deep, wide forest which is very famous in Brittany. In one part of the forest the fountain of Berenton springs forth beside a great stone. Once hunters made a practice of going to Berenton in hot weather, dipping out the water with their hunting horns, and wetting the top of the stone, which, according to custom, would cause rain. So it was the custom, long ago, to cause rain to fall in the forest and surrounding regions, but I don't know why it occurred. There too, if the Bretons are telling the truth, it was customary to see fairies and many other wonders. It was also usual to find gos-hawks' nests there, and large deer in abundance, but the peasants have destroyed them all. I went there seeking wonders; I saw the forest, and I saw the countryside; I looked for wonders, but I found none. A fool I returned, a fool I went; a fool I went, a fool I returned; I sought foolish things, and I think myself a fool"(*Le roman de Rou*, ed. H. Andresen, 2.6395–6420, as quoted in Jean Frappier, *Etude sur Yvain ou le chevalier au lion de Chrétien de Troyes*, Paris, Société d'Edition d'Enseignement Supérieur, 1969). Frappier notes that the fountain of Berenton still exists and is known by that name,

and that Brocéliande Forest is today the forest of Paimpont, located about 25 miles (40 kilometers) to the west of Rennes (*Etude sur Yvain*, p. 85).

185. The gentleman is a vavasor, a small landholder.

214. The silk is "escarlate," which Frappier says is a silk fabric, not a color (*Etude sur Yvain*, p. 229). Reto R. Bezzola notes in *Le sens de l'aventure et de l'amour* (*Chrétien de Troyes*) (Paris: Editions Champion, 1968), pp. 128–130, that the medieval listener was more apt to attribute a symbolic value to reality than is the twentieth-century reader and was accustomed to seeing a state of mind expressed in the color of clothing and the choice of precious stones. Red, a noble and festive color, symbolized love, valor, and glory: Yvain is dressed in scarlet red silk (vermeille) when he meets his future wife, who echoes the color in her red cushion (ll. 1740, 1803), and he is given clothes dyed red (greinne) by the lady of Noríson (l. 2797). Vair, a color derived from the spotted white fur on the underbelly of the grey squirrel and used to describe women's eyes (changing, blue-grey), animals (dappled or spotted), and fabrics (variegated), symbolized beauty or purity: Yvain is given a vair silk cloak to wear before he fights with the demons (l. 5186). Ermine and vair fur could be worn only by the nobility: Yvain's wife wears new ermine robes to greet King Arthur, and the rubies in her diadem assured their wearer of precedence, the highest place, and great love and favor, for the ruby was endowed with the powers of all the precious stones (l. 392). Of the other jewels mentioned in *Yvain*, the emerald, endowed in antiquity with rainmaking properties (l. 390), was highly prized for its green color (hope or new love) and symbolized unwavering faith (l. 5857); the jacinth, a yellow stone with a red tinge, assured its wearer of honor, happiness, a good welcome, favor with his host, protection from foul air, and an ability to resist intrigues (l. 5857).

363. Harris observes in his introduction to Chrétien de Troyes, *Yvain*, translated by André Mary, p. 33, that when the Celts were converted to Christianity, the priests insisted that they build chapels by the springs and fountains where they had formerly worshiped fairies and sprites.

430. The fountain, tree, and birds are united into one Other World landscape, similar to this landscape in *Yvain*, in the tenth-century *Navigatio Sancti Brendani* (*Voyage of Saint Brendan*), as Brown notes in *Iwain*, p. 86. A tree with a flock of birds singing in harmony beside a noble well appears in *Serglige Conculaind* (*The Sickbed of Cuchulainn*) (ibid., p. 39).

432. Frappier notes in *Etude sur Yvain*, p. 233, that the detailed description of the birds' polyphonic singing indicates Chrétien's interest in music.

537. The ending of Calogrenant's tale paraphrases Wace's account of his visit to the fountain of Berenton (see l. 177n).

557. Comfort mentions in Chrétien de Troyes, *Arthurian Romances*, p. 368, that Noradin is the Sultan Nureddin Mahmud (reigned 1146-1173), and that Forré is a legendary Saracen King of Naples, mentioned in the epic poems. Many scholars believe that this reference to Nureddin enables us to date the *Yvain* as having been

written before Nureddin's death in 1173. However Frappier assigns a later date to *Yvain;* he believes that it was written after 1176 and before 1181 and that the reference to Nureddin is a proverbial expression which remained in use after the Sultan's death (*Etude sur Yvain*, p. 16).

630. The feast day of Saint John the Baptist is June 24.

722. Since Yvain rides from Carduel in Wales to Brocéliande Forest in Brittany in two days, with no mention of crossing the Channel, it seems likely that Chrétien considered "Bretagne" a geographical unit for the purposes of this poem. Loomis suggests (*Arthurian Tradition*, p. 273) that a Breton minstrel substituted the name of the Breton forest and its famous fountain for a spring in the Blanche Lande, without changing the directions for reaching the domain of Duke Laududez (or Laudunez) in Scotland. This inconsistency in detail would not have troubled medieval listeners.

835. Frappier notes (*Etude sur Yvain*, pp. 75–76) that the simile of the falcon and the crane was inspired by a passage from Ovid's *Metamorphoses* (1.533) which describes a hound chasing a hare. Another image inspired by Ovid occurs in Gawain's speech (ll. 2353–2356) about love postponed being like a green log: Ovid, in *Ars amatoria* (*Art of Love*), 2.573–575, contrasts the young man's impetuous passion with the longer lasting love of the older man.

895. Brown observes that there are many parallels between the Celtic tale of *Gilla Decair* (*Slothful Gillie*) and this section of *Yvain* (*Iwain*, pp. 104–106 and 115–116). In *Slothful Gillie* are the following: the passage through tangled woods and briars (l. 173), a markedly similar description of the herdsman (ll. 264 and 670ff), the landscape of a tree with interlaced boughs by a bubbling spring, stone, gold drinking vessel, and singing birds (ll. 380–390), and a warrior clad in red (ll. 447 and 1821) who makes a noise like an army, leads the hero through a town to a palace, and leaves the hero shut outside the doors (ll. 822–895).

953. Gustave Cohen says in *Chrétien de Troyes et son oeuvre* (Paris: Joseph Flock, Maître Imprimeur à Moyenne, no. 50 Dépôt légal, 1er trimestre 1948), pp. 352–353, that the magic ring reflects the ring of Gygès and the ring which Medea gave to Jason in the *Roman de Troie*.

1076. Frappier points out (*Etude sur Yvain*, pp. 73–75) that the description of the widow's dramatic grief may have been inspired by Ovid's advice in *Art of Love* 3.431–432: "Often it happens that at the funeral of one husband, one finds another. The widow should walk with her hair unbound and should not prevent her tears from flowing freely." Yvain's observation "women have one hundred hearts" (l. 1330) is inspired by the same work of Ovid (ibid., 1.755–756) as is the idea of enlisting the aid of the lady's handmaiden.

1090. Comfort states that this passage contains the earliest known literary reference to cruentation, or the belief that a dead man's wounds would bleed afresh in the presence of his murderer (Chrétien de Troyes, *Arthurian Romances*, pp. 369–370).

1176. The mark had the value of one-half pound of silver, according to Reid in Chrétien de Troyes, *Yvain* (Foerster), p. 242.

1253. Yvain falls in love with the lady in the tradition of courtly love, whose rules were codified later by Andreas Capellanus. The lady's beauty inspires Yvain's love, as Yvain's noble birth and courage inspire the lady's love later in the romance. The descriptions of Love striking Yvain's heart through his eyes (l. 1264), his languor (l. 1427), his fear in her presence (l. 1804), and his complete submission to the lady's will (ll. 1829, 4373–4374, and 6476–6477) are traditional.

1672. Swift remarriage, and even remarriage with one's husband's murderer, were not uncommon during the warlike periods of the Middle Ages. Among other literary precedents is the marriage of Oedipus and Jocasta in the *Roman de Thèbes* and the ancient motif of slaying the mate of a fertility goddess and replacing him with a new mate.

1676. Frappier notes in *Etude sur Yvain*, p. 207, that Chrétien wishes to attach Yvain to the symbolic lineage of Abel, that is, of the Just.

1741. Frappier states in *Etude sur Yvain*, p. 121, that chalk was used to preserve furs in the Middle Ages.

1943. W. L. Holland observes that this thought is repeated in Shakespeare's *King Henry IV*, part 1, act 5, scene 4:

> When that this body did contain a spirit,
> A kingdom for it was too small a bound,
> But now two paces of the vilest earth
> Is room enough.

(Comfort's notes in Chrétien de Troyes, *Arthurian Romances*, p. 370.)

2005. Loomis says in *Arthurian Tradition*, pp. 302–303, that the lady of Landuc is not named in seven of the nine manuscripts of *Yvain*, including the Guiot copy. In one manuscript she is called Laudine, and in the other Laudune. "Leudonia" or "Laudonia" is the name of the district of Lothian in Scotland.

2517ff. Instead of attending King Arthur's court, Yvain and Gawain have established their own court, which indicates that their pride has become excessive.

2653. Frappier notes in *Etude sur Yvain*, p. 78, that Chrétien was greatly influenced by the Tristan legend, and that traces of it appear in many incidents of *Yvain*. Yvain's life in the forest and encounter with the hermit recall Tristan's existence in the Forest of Morois. Lunette's betrayal by the seneschal and sentence to death by fire recall Iseut's persecutions. The threat of handing Gawain's niece over to the filthy lackeys echoes the incident of Iseut and the lepers. Yvain's rescue of three hundred captives is written in a literary tradition which includes Tristan's rescue of Mark's subjects from Morholt of Ireland.

2655. Yvain's food symbolizes his gradual rehabilitation.

2677. The old French monetary table resembled the old English monetary table: 12 deniers equaled 1 sol; 20 sous equaled 1 livre (Comfort, in Chrétien de Troyes, *Arthurian Romances*, p. 370). *Denier* is translated as "penny" and *sol* as "shilling" to clarify the relative values of these coins.

2774. In the Arthurian legends, Morgan the Fay, a fairy, is the sister of King Arthur.

2825. Brown maintains in *Iwain*, p. 44, that there are striking parallels between *Yvain* and the Celtic tale *The Sickbed of Cuchulainn*. In both tales the heroes journey to an Other World landscape after hearing the tale of a previous adventurer, enter the Other World landscape through a perilous passage, are protected by the lady's confidante, and are smitten by the lady's beauty. Afterward both heroes break their promises and become insane as a result of being rejected by the lady, and both heroes are cured of their madness by a magic remedy.

3039. The forest of Argonne lies on the borders of Champagne and Lorraine.

3047. This passage refers to the *Song of Roland;* Durendal is Roland's sword.

3162. Brown notes in *Iwain*, p. 132, that Foerster suggests that the meeting with the lion has its source in the tale of Androcles and the lion and that Gaidoz infers that the theme was brought from the Orient. In connection with Gaidoz's theory, Brown mentions Jaufré de Vigeois's tale of a crusader, Golfier de las Tours, of whom the story was told that he saved a lion from a serpent and was afterward followed and aided by the lion.

3170. Frappier observes in *Etude sur Yvain*, p. 214, that the lion occupies a high position in the "moralizing" hierarchy of the *Bestiaries:* as the symbol of nobility and power, the lion is the antithesis of the serpent, symbol of treachery and wickedness. In the mystical order the lion became an allegorical figure of Christ and in the profane order an allegorical figure of the perfect knight.

3321. Harris says that this scene of the lion's suicide attempt is a parody of the Pyramus and Thisbe legend (Chrétien de Troyes, *Yvain*, translated by André Mary, p. 151).

3511. This passage is the first of three allusions to Chrétien de Troyes's preceding romance *Lancelot*. In the incident to which Lunette refers, a knight named Meleagant announces at King Arthur's court that he holds many knights and maidens of Arthur's domain as his captives. If the king has any knight whom he would trust to escort the queen, and who is able to protect her from Meleagant, the prisoners will be freed. Kay threatens to leave court unless the king grants him a favor, and the king promises to grant Kay's request without first learning what it will be. Kay asks permission to accept Meleagant's challenge, and the king, who has been tricked into giving his word, is forced to consent. The queen departs reluctantly with Kay, who is unhorsed, and Meleagant leads the queen away as his captive.

Gawain and Lancelot set out to rescue the queen. Lancelot, inspired by his secret love for the queen, surpasses Gawain, the perfect knight, and after many dangers and humiliations Lancelot rescues the queen and sees his love rewarded. But Meleagant deceives Lancelot and walls him up in a tower, and it is Gawain who returns the queen to court. Eventually Lancelot escapes from the tower, returns to court, and kills Meleagant in combat. See lines 3712–3734 and 4517–4523 for other allusions to *Lancelot*.

3890. The dwarf, like the seneschal, is often portrayed as a villain. In a society which equated physical and moral qualities in its literature, the ugly and misshapen were presumed to be wicked unless, as in the case of the Giant Herdsman, proven otherwise.

4068. Brown notes in *Iwain*, pp. 130–131, that the Welsh Owain was linked with helpful animals, his lion and his ravens, and that since shields were emblazoned frequently with the device of a lion, Yvain may have been known as the Knight of the Lion before Chrétien wrote his romance. "Le chevalier au lion" is translated as "the knight with the lion" because the preposition conveys an important idea of the romance: that Yvain and his lion were comrades-in-arms.

4220. This passage expresses the theory of the judicial trial by combat.

4510. Overgenerously Gawain has promised to do as the elder sister requests without first learning what it will be. When he realizes the injustice of the cause he has promised to defend, he decides to fight in disguise and swears the elder sister to secrecy.

4872ff. In one of the most important passages of the romance, Yvain shows that he realizes he owes his strength and his victories to God.

4965. Cohen notes in *Chrétien de Troyes*, p. 342, that the poverty of the three hundred maidens reflects the poverty of the textile workers in certain regions of Champagne or Artois. On the other hand, Loomis, in *Arthurian Tradition*, mentions Professor Hall's belief that the description of the maidens reflects the employment conditions of Christian slave girls in the Moslem world (p. 323).

5034. The devil's sons are neutons: the offspring of a woman and an incubus. Merlin was similarly conceived.

5063ff. Reid says in Chrétien de Troyes, *Yvain* (Foerster), p. 212, that each maidens' handwork, when sold, earns a princely income of twenty shillings, but she receives only fourpence (one-sixtieth of this sum) in wages, from which she must pay for food and clothing. The difference is going to the owner of the castle, whose profits are enormous.

5520. Cohen observes in *Chrétien de Troyes*, p. 341, that the rescue of the captive maidens recalls the legends of Theseus rescuing Athenian captives from the Minotaur and of Tristan rescuing Mark's subjects from Morholt.

5732. The Love-Hate debate is a magnificent example of the use of dialectic reasoning in replying to the kind of question posed at the courts of love.

5831. Brown points out in *Iwain*, p. 17, that the combat between Yvain and Gawain is written in the tradition of the combat of fratres jurati (sworn brothers).

6337. Frappier notes in *Etude sur Yvain*, p. 57, that, judging from the context, "Truth" seems to have been a parlor game played in courtly circles in which someone was induced to swear an oath or undertake some task without realizing all the implications or consequences.

BIBLIOGRAPHY

Andreas Capellanus. *The Art of Courtly Love*. Introduction, translation, and notes by John Jay Parry. New York: Columbia University Press, 1941.

Bezzola, Reto R. *Le sens de l'aventure et de l'amour (Chrétien de Troyes)*. Paris: Editions Champion, 1968.

Brown, Arthur Charles Lewis. *Iwain: Study in the Origins of Arthurian Romance*. New York: Haskell House, 1968.

Chrétien de Troyes. *Arthurian Romances*. Translated by W. Wistar Comfort. Everyman's Library, no. 98. London: J. M. Dent and Sons, 1914.

———. *Le chevalier au lion (Yvain)*. Edited by Mario Roques. Paris: Editions Champion, 1967.

———. *Le chevalier de la charrette*. Edited by Mario Roques. Paris: Editions Champion, 1970.

———. *Yvain (le chevalier au lion)*. Critical text of Wendelin Foerster. Introduction, notes, and glossary by T. B. W. Reid. Manchester: Manchester University Press, 1942.

———. *Yvain; ou le chevalier au lion*. Prepared by Jan Nelson and Carleton W. Carroll. Introduction by Douglas Kelly. New York: Appleton-Century Crofts, 1968.

———. *Yvain, ou le chevalier au lion*. Translated by André Mary. Introduction and notes by Julian Harris. New York: Dell, 1963.

———. *Ywain, the Knight of the Lion*. Translated by Robert W. Ackerman and Frederick W. Locke. New York: Frederick Ungar, 1957.

Cohen, Gustave. *Chrétien de Troyes et son oeuvre*. Paris: Joseph Flock, Maître Imprimeur à Moyenne, no. 50 Dépôt légal, 1er trimestre, 1948.

Frappier, Jean. *Chrétien de Troyes*. Paris: Hatier, "Connaissance des Lettres," 1957.

———. *Etude sur Yvain ou le chevalier au lyon de Chrétien de Troyes*. Paris: Société d'Edition d'Enseignement Supérieur, 1969.

Harris, Julian. "The Role of the Lion in Chrétien de Troyes' *Yvain*," *PMLA* 54 (1949): 1143–1163.

Holmes, Urban T. *Chrétien de Troyes*. New York: Twayne, 1970.

Jackson, W. T. H. *The Literature of the Middle Ages*. New York: Columbia University Press, 1960.

Loomis, Roger Sherman. *Arthurian Tradition and Chrétien de Troyes*. New York: Columbia University Press, 1949.

———. *The Development of Arthurian Romance*. London: Hutchinson, 1963.

The Mabinogion. Translated by Gwyn Jones and Thomas Jones. Everyman's Library. London: J. M. Dent and Sons, 1949.

Malory, Thomas. *Le morte d'Arthur*. Translated by Keith Baines. New York: Mentor Classics, 1962.

Morte Arthur. Everyman's Library, no. 634. London: J. M. Dent and Sons, 1936.

Nitze, William A. "Yvain and the Myth of the Fountain." *Speculum* 30 (1955): 170–179.

Reason, Joseph H. *An Inquiry into the Structural Style and Originality of Chrestien's Yvain.* Studies in Romance Languages and Literatures, no. 57. Washington, D.C.: Catholic University of America Press, 1958.

Wace. *Le roman de Brut.* Edited by Ivor Arnold. Vol. 2. Paris: Société des Anciens Textes Français, 1940.

——— and Layamon. *Arthurian Chronicles.* Everyman's Library, no. 578. London: J. M. Dent and Sons, 1937.

Wilczynski, Massimila Ines. *The Sources and Analogues of Chrétien's Yvain.* Chicago: University of Chicago Press, 1943.